Robert Pęc

Colour illustr
Teodor Liviu Morosanu

North American
P-51D/K
& CAC Mustang

STRATUS

Published in Poland in 2009
by STRATUS s.c.
Po. Box 123,
27-600 Sandomierz 1, Poland
e-mail: office@mmpbooks.biz
for
Mushroom Model Publications,
3 Gloucester Close, Petersfield,
Hampshire GU32 3AX, UK.
e-mail: rogerw@mmpbooks.biz

http://www.mmpbooks.biz

ISBN
978-83-89450-60-9

Editor in chief
Roger Wallsgrove

Editorial Team
Bartłomiej Belcarz
Artur Juszczak
James Kightly
Robert Pęczkowski

DTP
Robert Pęczkowski
Artur Juszczak

Colour Drawings
Teodor Liviu Morosanu
Scale Plans
Dariusz Karnas

Additional Walkround
Captions & Research
James Kightly

Printed by:
Drukarnia Diecezjalna,
ul. Żeromskiego 4,
27-600 Sandomierz
tel. (15) 832 31 92;
fax (15) 832 77 87
www.wds.pl marketing@wds.pl

PRINTED IN POLAND

Table of contents

Acknowledgements: (for written accounts and materials):
Peter Anderson, Steve Atkin, Arthur Bentley, Brett Clowes, Randall Haskin, Mike Jerram, David Jones, RAAF Museum Archive, Wojtek Matusiak, Arthur Lochte, Archive Svensk Flyghitorisk Förening, Dariusz Karnas, Airshow Traveler, Malcolm Laird.

We would also like to record our thanks to those who have made available their Mustangs for the photographs illustrating this book. The accuracy and authenticity of restorations has recently improved to a very high standard. Where possible, we have outlined where markings and details are typical and accurate to wartime appearance. Equally, where there are deviations from the original, we have tried to call these out as well. However, the reader is advised that the study of Mustang details can be an endless and detailed work, sometimes without 'definitive' answers.

Special thanks:
We have been privileged to be able to compliment the original W.W.II North American Aviation pictures supplied by Mike Jerram with extensive colour details of the Midwest Aero Restorations Mustang rebuild, for Bruce Winter, of 'Happy Jack's Go Buggy' (P-51D-30NA 44-74452, N74190). The term 'benchmark' is often over-used, but this restoration is both to the highest quality and also, more critically for us, as accurate as current, extensive research can make it. In terms of P-51D restorations, it is a benchmark of a recreated original appearance. (There are museum Mustangs that have unrestored original structure and fittings, but as far as we are aware, there are none as complete as this one.) Thanks to Mike Vanboncouer of Midwest, we have been able to use restoration photographs with detail only available via the restoration team, and insights based on Mike's extensive research and knowledge, as well as more excellent photographs by Steve Atkin and James P Church of this aircraft. Steve Atkin has also provided photographs of the detail work being carried out on Peter Teichman's 'Jumpin Jaques' (P-51D-20NA, G-SIJJ) to a similar standard.

Introduction

The history of the design and development of the iconic P-51 Mustang is so well known that it is superfluous to repeat much of the story here. To summarise, the British Purchasing commission approached North American Aviation (NAA) early in 1940 to build Curtiss P-40s under licence for the RAF, as Curtiss had insufficient capacity to meet the urgent British requirements. NAA made a counter proposal, to design and build a better fighter using the same Allison engine, in much the same time as would be needed to tool up for P-40 production. There had already been preliminary design work on such a fighter, making use of some data from Curtiss relating to their projected P-46 design. In the event, the ensuing NA-73 design owed little to the P-46, apart from the ventral radiator which was carefully designed to minimise drag (and ultimately proved capable of delivering some net thrust). One novel feature of the NA-73 was the use of a laminar-flow wing section, as designed by NACA. The overall design was a model of aerodynamic cleanliness, for the time, and the prototype proved significantly faster than the P-40 using an identical engine. In addition, the aircraft had an excellent range (the perennial weakness of British fighters, from the '30s to the '60s!).

The first production NA-73 Mustang with British serial AG345. Serial was painted on the rudder and under the port and above starboard wing. ***(Mike Jerram via Roger Wallsgrove)***

The next production NA-73 in British camouflage. *(NAA)*

The RAF happily ordered the new design, named "Mustang", and these Allison-powered aircraft served very effectively in the army cooperation, reconnaissance and ground attack roles from 1942 onwards. They were not used much by Fighter Command as the Mustang had poor performance at medium to high altitudes compared to the Spitfire and opposing German fighters. The USAAF belatedly realised the potential of the design, and ordered some as the P-51 and A-36, the latter a dive-bomber variant.

In both Britain and the USA it was realised by mid 1942 that the full potential of the design could not be exploited with the Allison engine. Rolls-Royce fitted Merlin engines to several Mustangs under the designation Mustang Mk.X, and NAA made similar trials using Packard-built Merlins. The first Mustang X flew in October 1942, and the Merlin-powered P-51B followed in November. The results were dramatic, with much improved altitude performance and climb rate, and even before these test flights the USAAF had ordered the P-51B in quantity.

The P-51B and P-51C (the latter essentially identical but built at the Dallas plant) featured a deeper radiator bath, incorporating the intercooler, and intake scoops under the nose rather than above as on the Allison aircraft (feeding updraught rather than downdraught carburettors), and wing mounted armament of 4 x .50 cal Browning machine guns. These aircraft equipped 8th Air Force fighter units in Britain, who for the first time could provide fighter escort for the B-17s and B-24s even as far as Berlin (once the aircraft were fitted with fuselage fuel tanks and drop tanks under the wings). The RAF took delivery of P-51Bs and -Cs as the Mustang III from 1944.

The Mustang was now an excellent long-range escort fighter, a match for any Luftwaffe opposition, but there were problems. Rear visibility was very poor with the original canopy design, only partly alleviated by the "Malcolm hood" designed and fitted in Britain to many Mustang IIIs. The armament was also relatively light (half that of the P-47 Thunderbolt). Hawker in Britain had begun fitting their Typhoon fighter-bomber with a "bubble" canopy with unrestricted all-round vision, and similar canopies were tested on both the P-51 and P-47. Enter the P-51D ...

P-51B with British serial FX982 in British camouflage, but with American markings. ***(Stratus coll.)***

P-51D/K

The P-51D Mustang with bubble canopy was the best-known version of the Mustang. It was also the most widely used variant of the Mustang, with a total of 8102 machines of this type produced, 6502 at Inglewood and 1600 in Dallas.

The P-51B and P-51C were excellent aircraft that served until the end of the war, but B and C models suffered poor rear visibility and gun jamming during high-G manoeuvres. Also the B/C versions only had four .50 cal Brownings (2 in each wing). NAA also took the opportunity to make other improvements to the new version.

The British had figured out how to make a bubble or "teardrop" canopy with 360° view and they were beginning to use them on the latest model of Spitfires and Typhoons. The U.S. Army sent Col. Mark Bradley to England in January of 1943 to learn the workings of this new canopy and then find a way to get them on U.S. fighters. Bradley returned and began to incorporate the new style. The first U.S. fighter so tested was a Republic P-47.

NA-102, P-51B-1 NA, 43-12102 with bubble canopy, the next two NA-102 were finished as NA-106, P-51D. The last three digits of the serial were repeated on the nose. ***(Mike Jerram via Roger Wallsgrove)***

A P-51B-1 (43-12102) was selected to be modified as the test aircraft for the new bubble canopy and was designated NA-109. The new shaped canopy gave almost completely unobstructed all-round vision with virtually no distortion from the free-blown glazing. The plexiglas of the hood was mounted on rubber in a metal frame, the sill around the bottom being very deep. The canopy was manually opened and closed by a hand crank operated by the pilot. To accommodate the new canopy, the rear fuselage of the Mustang had to be cut down, but the amount of retooling needed to accomplish this was not extensive. This modified P-51B took off on its first flight at Inglewood on 17 November 1943, with test pilot Bob Chilton at the controls.

With the success of 43-12102, NAA modified the next two P-51B-10NA serials 43-106539 and 43-106540 as NA-106 (order dated May 1, 1943) with the bubble canopy and the six .50 cal guns. These aircraft were initially designated as XP-51D and later changed to P-51D-NA. These aircraft were also powered with the same engine as the P-51B/C – the Packard V-1650-7.

The gun installation was completely redesigned, to accommodate installation of three MG53-2 0.50 in machine guns in each wing, all of them mounted upright and all fed by ammunition belts. The arrangement of the ammo chutes eliminated the jamming problem of the B/C models. The inner gun carried 400 rounds and the two outer guns had 280 rounds each.

The gear operation was also changed and this led to the increase of the wing root chord. The aileron effectiveness and strength were both improved. A seal was added to the leading edge of the aileron which helped ease stick pressure during high speed manoeuvres. The landing light was also moved from the wing leading edge to inside the landing gear well.

The extra long-range tank behind the pilot exacerbated an existing problem with yaw stability. Also, problems had been encountered with snap-rolls causing a structural failure of the horizontal stabiliser on the P-51B/C and D models. As a solution, the P-51D had a dorsal fin fillet added to the fuselage-vertical stabiliser join. The fillet was also added to other P-51 models already in the field.

Port side of P-51B-1, 43-12102 with bubble canopy. Aircraft awaiting flights trials.
(Mike Jerram via Roger Wallsgrove)

Production series

The first batch of P-51Ds was the -1-NA block, factory designation NA-110. These 100 P-51Ds were delivered unassembled to Australia. The first four aircraft in this block still had the B model canopy.

NA-109 was the order placed in July of 1943 for 2,500 P-51s.

The first block of P-51D-5-NA had 800 aircraft,

The second block, P-51D-5-NA, comprised 800 aircraft.

P-51D-10-NA – 800 aircraft.

The dorsal fin was added during the production run. This dorsal was retrofied to older aircraft.

P-51D-15-NA - 400 aircraft.

P-51D-15-NA - 500 aircraft.

Continued on page 14.

P-51D-5, 44-13366, in flight, without the dorsal fillet.
(Mike Jerram via Roger Wallsgrove)

1/72 P-51D-5.

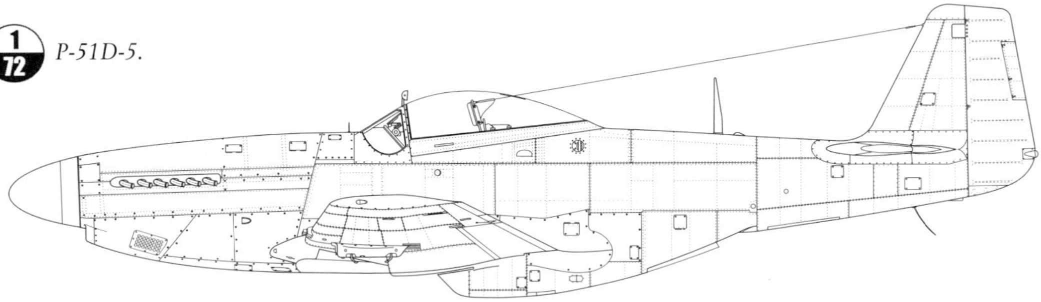

A very famous shot of a CAC Mustang Mk.20 of 3 Squadron RAAF running-up with a lot of dust at Darwin, NT. This aircraft has five rather than three rocket launchers on each wing. **(RAAF Museum archive)**

P-51D-10-NA, 44-14214 with fillet. **(Mike Jerram via Roger Wallsgrove)**

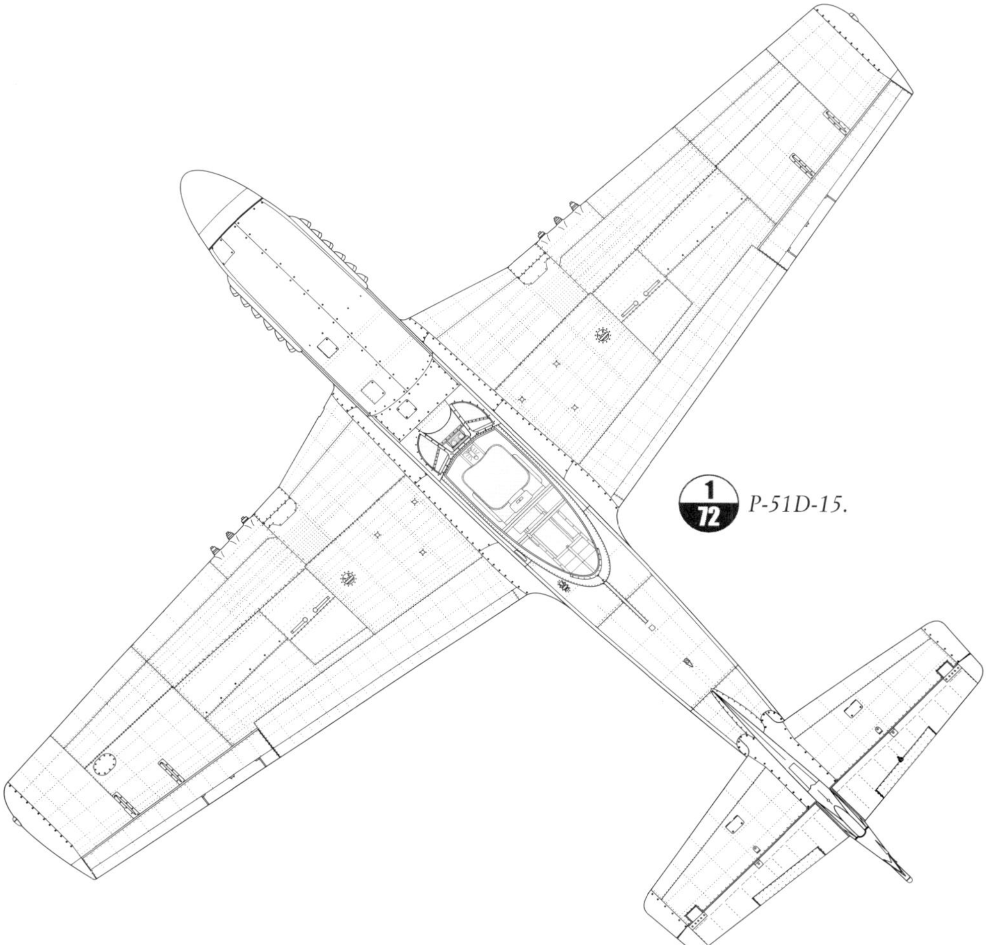

1/72 P-51D-15.

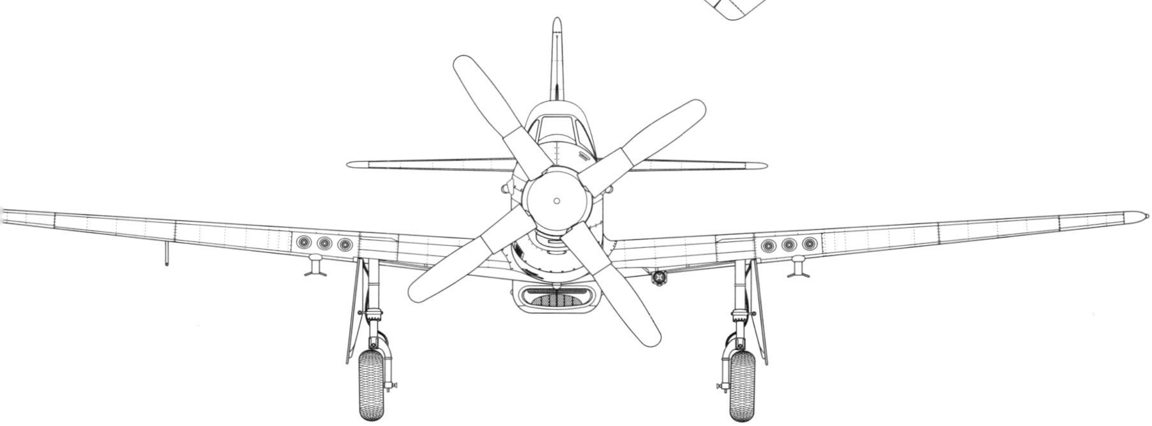

1/72 *P-51D-15.*

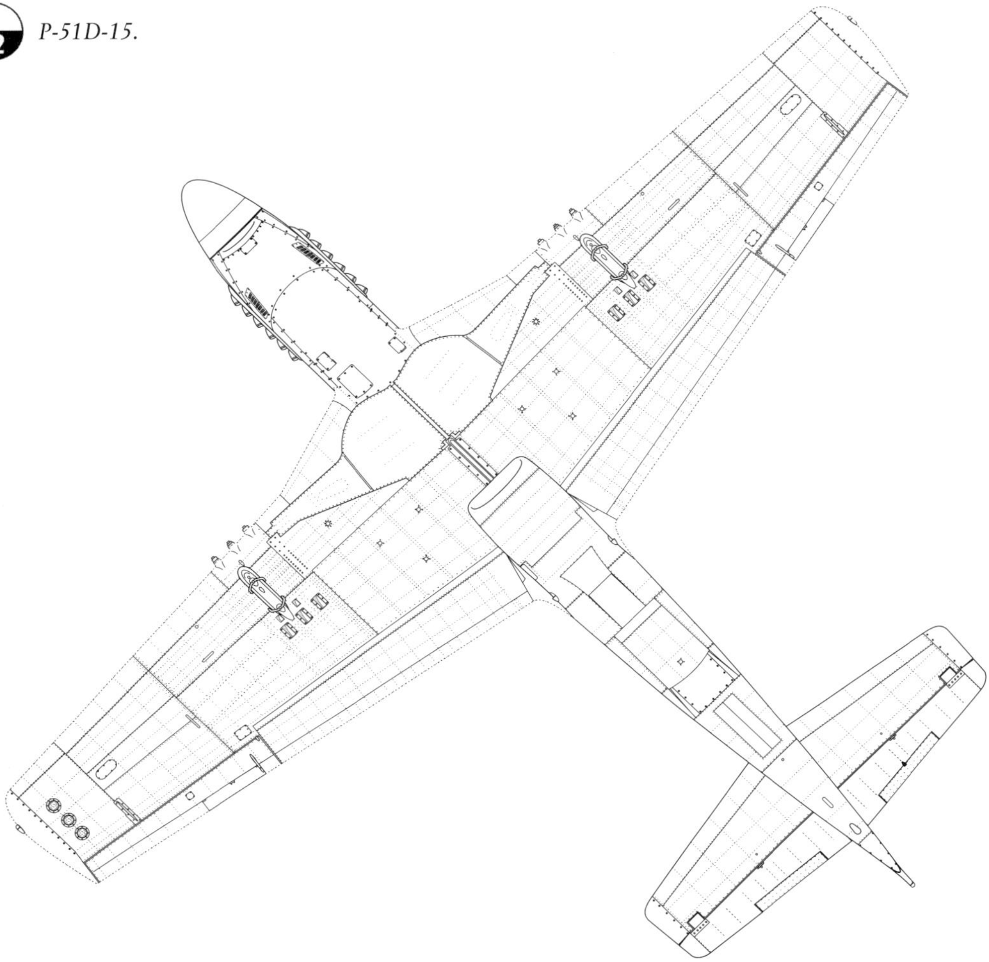

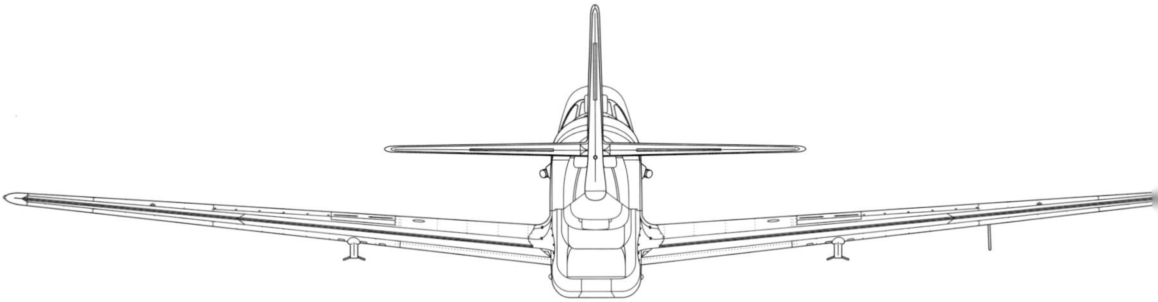

NAA factory in Inglewood. Model batches NA-109 and NA-122 were built simultaneously. *(See page 14 for details.)* *(**Mike Jerram via Roger Wallsgrove**)*

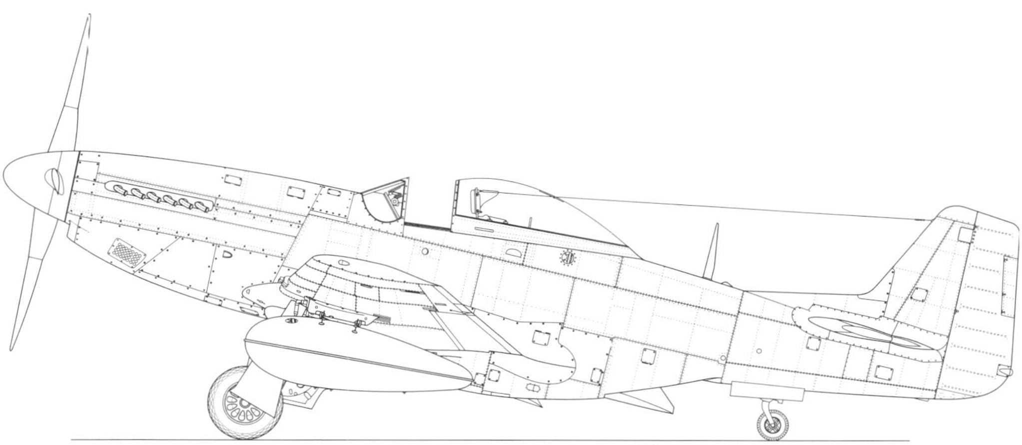

1/72 *P-51D-15 with 75 gallon drop tanks.*

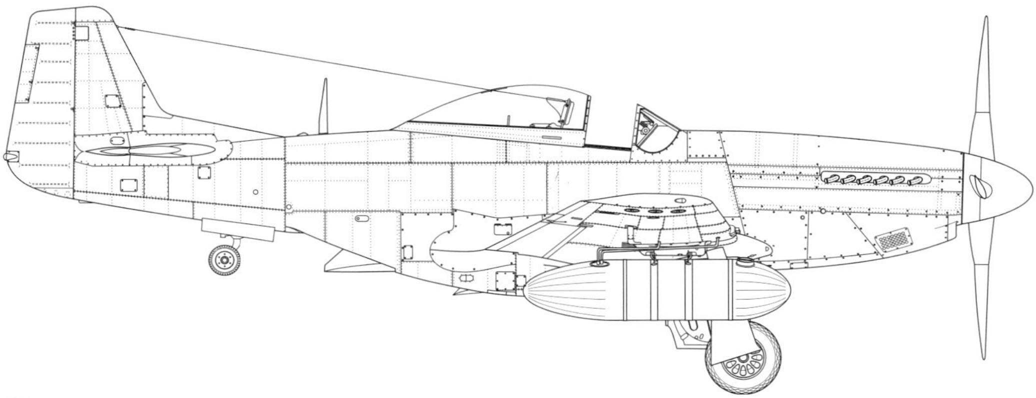

1/72 P-51D-15 with 110 gallon impregnated paper drop tanks.

Lines of P-51D-10-NAs at the factory airfield awaiting delivery to combat units.
(Mike Jerram via Roger Wallsgrove)

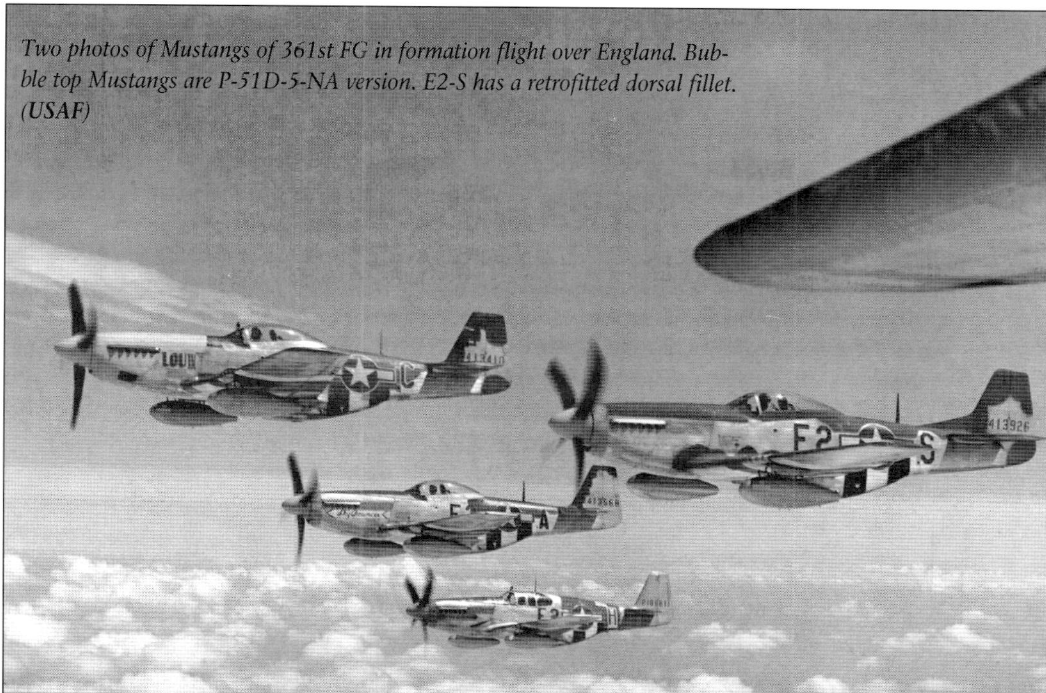

Two photos of Mustangs of 361st FG in formation flight over England. Bubble top Mustangs are P-51D-5-NA version. E2-S has a retrofitted dorsal fillet. (USAF)

In June of 1944 an additional order was placed for 4,000 P-51Ds. This order was designated NA-122. The production blocks of NA-122 were:

P-51D-20-NA – 1,000 aircraft.

P-51D-20-NA - 100 aircraft.
The K-14 gun sight was introduced in October 1944. This gun sight was based on a British (Ferranti) design.

P-51D-20-NA - 500 aircraft, metal covered elevators were introduced in February 1945.

P-51D-25-NA – 1,000 aircraft, with attachment points for various forms of rockets and rocket launchers.

P-51D-25-NA - 600 aircraft

P-51D-30-NA - 800 aircraft

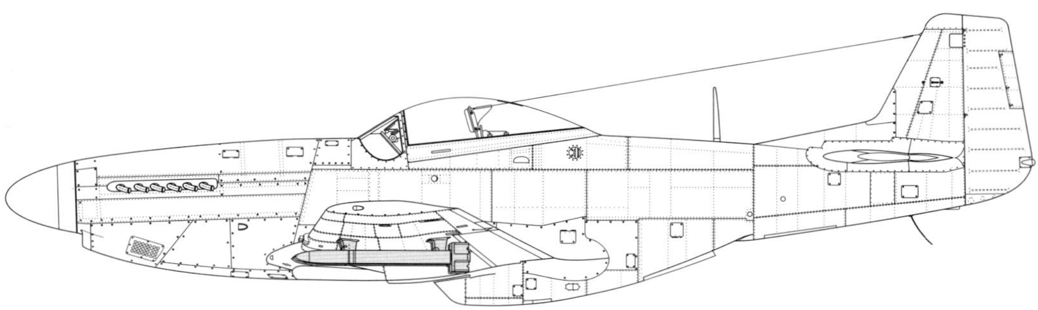

1/72 *P-51D-25 with rockets and AN/APS-13 warning radar.*

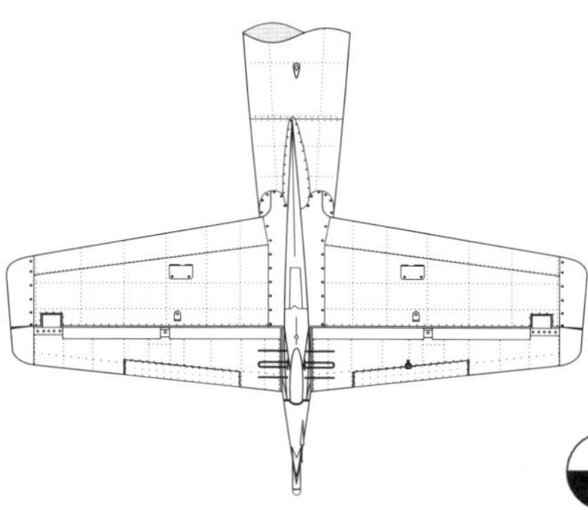

1/72 *Horizontal stabiliser with metal covered elevators. AN/APS-13 warning radar is also shown.*

1/72

P-51D-25 with special aerials used for long distance flight over the Pacific.

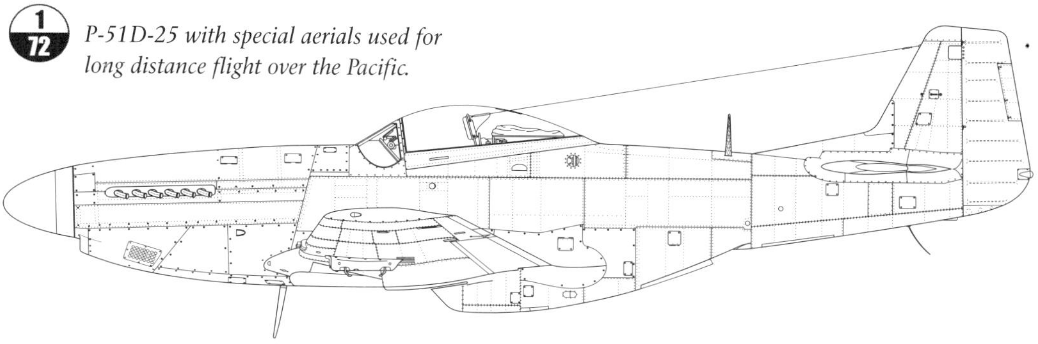

When the P-51D began production, once again the Dallas plant was needed. Unlike the B variant, when the P-51Ds were built in Dallas, their designation of "D" was kept. They were identified as built at the Dallas plant with the "NT" suffix. So a -5 block of a P-51D built in Dallas would be a P-51D-5NT, identical to a P-51D-5NA built in Inglewood.

At the Dallas NAA plant, 1,600 P-51D models were produced.
NA-111:
P-51D-5-NT – 200 aircraft
P-51D-20-NT – 400 aircraft.

Order for NA-124 included:
P-51D-25-NT – 600 aircraft
P-51D-30-NT – 400 aircraft.

Seen at Speke, Liverpool airport, the aircraft in foreground is a F-6K at the end of WWII. Mustang 44-12527 had served with the 69th TRG in the ETO and, rather than returning to the US, found its way to Germany after the war as part of the Occupation Air Force.

(USAF)

F-6K-10-NT at airfield in England. **(Stratus coll.)**

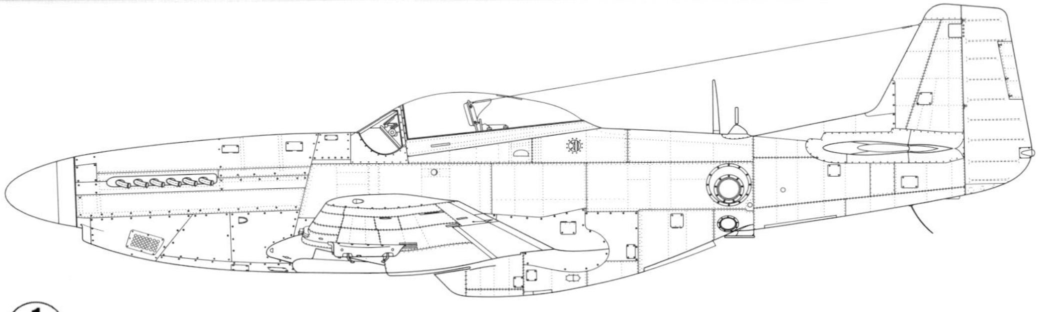

1/72 F-6D.

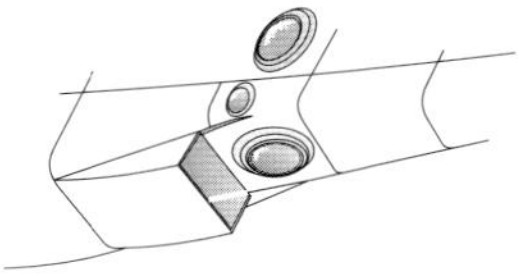

F-6.

Aircraft for conversion to the photo reconnaissance version of P-51D were taken from both the Inglewood and Dallas plants and designated F-6D. ('F' standing for 'Foto'.)

F-6D-20-NT – 31 aircraft,

F-6D-25-NT – 70 aircraft

F-6D-30-NT – 35 aircraft

The F-6 had cameras mounted in the rear fuselage, one facing to the pilot's left and slightly forward and a camera facing downward out of the bottom of the fuselage. Most F-6s retained their armament

Dual Control P-51Ds

There have been three primary types of dual-control P-51s used by militaries throughout the world. The principal reason for dual control aircraft is to train pilots both to fly the Mustang and to use it as a weapon.

TP-51

The TP-51D was a two-seat, dual control aircraft built by North American Aviation simultaneous to the 1940s production run of the P-51D. The fuselage tank was removed and the radio gear and battery were relocated.

TP-51D-NT, 44-84610 in flight. (**Stratus coll.**)

A rear seat with full dual-controls was added, but the rear seat only featured rudimentary cockpit instrumentation. Unlike the later TEMCO TF-51Ds, these airframes used a standard P-51D/K canopy and did not have a redesigned aft fuselage area. There were ten TP-51Ds produced:

TP-51D-NT serial numbers: 44-84610, 44-84611 and 45-11443 to 45-11450.

TEMCO TF-51D

In the early 1950s the US Air Force saw a need for additional dual control Mustangs. The USAF contracted with the Texas Engineering and Manufacturing Company (TEMCO) to modify 15 1944-model P-51Ds into dual control trainers. (The designation of these aircraft was TF-51D, reflecting the 1948 change in designation of 'Pursuit' aircraft to 'Fighter'). Unlike the NAA TP-51Ds, the TEMCO TF-51Ds featured a more significant design change to the P-51, incorporating a modified aft fuselage and an enlarged canopy. This allowed for a fully instrumented rear cockpit and headroom for the pilot who sat there.

TEMCO TF-51D: serial numbers 44-84654 to 44-84658, 44-84660, 44-84662, 44-84663, 44-84665 to 44-84670 and 44-84676.

Cavalier TF-51D

Cavalier Aircraft Corporation of Sarasota, Florida, built seven Cavalier TF-51Ds in the late 1960s and early 1970s. These aircraft did not officially serve with the US Air Force, but were constructed as trainers for countries who had been given Cavalier-modified Mustangs as military aid from the United States. The Cavalier TF-51Ds were very similar to the TEMCO design, but added features like a taller vertical stabiliser and numerous minor structural, mechanical, and cockpit improvements. Cavalier constructed their TF-51Ds out of surplus single-seat P-51D and P-51K airframes, but at least one was built from a former TEMCO fuselage and re-serial numbered. Due to the circumstances under which the Cavalier TF-51Ds were purchased, some of them received new USAF serials when rebuilt and some did not.

Cavalier TF-51D: 67-14866, 67-22582, 69-6599, FAS 400 (this is the El Salvador Air Force ID of the aircraft – it was not given a new USAF Serial number when it was constructed), 72-1536, 44-73260, and 44-84745.

Current civilian dual-control P-51Ds

In the last part of the 20th century, it became popular for P-51s to be converted to dual control during their 'restoration'. Several companies specializing in P-51 restoration performed these modifications using a mix of the TEMCO and Cavalier design features. There are also many two-seat P-51D machines flying today with partial controls fitted for the back seat occupant, however these do not normally have the full instrumentation of the proper TF-51 and are externally identical to the single-seat version they have been modified from.

P-51K Mustang. **(Stratus coll.)**

P-51K Mustang

The P-51K Mustang was a simply P-51D with a different propeller. Wartime production of the Hamilton Standard unit was not keeping up with demand and a suitable replacement was needed. Aeroproducts was contracted to supply the Dallas plant with 4-blade 11' diameter hollow steel propeller. All P-51K versions were initially fitted with this propeller when built, but it could be changed to the Hamilton Standard unit in service. (And, rarely, vice-versa.) While the aircraft was otherwise identical to the P-51D, many P-51K canopies look different due to a higher rear part of the bubble. The 'Dallas' canopy shape was due to different sub-contractors to NAA. The canopies were blown into shape and while setting up the Dallas production line, the shape of the canopy for the Ks was slightly changed for additional sub-contractors, allowing a bit more headroom for the pilots. Early Ks had the same (original) type installed as the Ds coming off the line at Inglewood, CA. (K models were built in Dallas, and D models in Inglewood.)

Also at the Inglewood, CA, line, at one stage a slightly different shaped canopy type was introduced, similar to the 'Dallas' type.

The P-51K production numbers were as follows: (factory designation NA-111)
P-51K-1-NT - 200
P-51K-5-NT - 400
P-51K-10-NT - 600
P-51K-15-NT - 200
P-51K-15-NT - 100.

163 of the K models were modified for the reconnaissance, designated F-6K and produced as follows:
F6K-5-NT - 57
F6K-1-0NT – 63
F6K-15-NT - 43.

The P-51D remained in service in considerable numbers with the USAAF for many years after the war. In 1948, the newly-formed USAF eliminated the P-for-pursuit category and replaced it with F-for-fighter. The designation of the P-51 was changed to F-51. In addition, the old category of F for photographic reconnaissance was eliminated, and F-6D and F-6K photographic reconnaissance aircraft became RF-51D and RF-51K respectively. Two seat TP-51D trainers became the TF-51D type. In RAF and Commonwealth service the P-51D family were known as the Mustang Mk.IV from the start.

The last American active-duty Mustang was P-51D-30-NA c/n 44-74936, which was finally withdrawn from service with the West Virginia ANG in 1957. This airplane is now on display at the National Museum of the USAF in Dayton, Ohio. It is, however, painted as P-51D-15-NA c/n 44-1517.

The CAC Mustang

Australia was the only country to licence-produce any version of the Mustang. In 1943, the Australian government arranged for the Commonwealth Aircraft Corporation (CAC) in Melbourne Victoria to build the P-51D, selected as the next fighter type to be produced for Australia. The RAAF urgently needed a new fighter, and so the first CAC Mustangs were built mainly from imported semi-finished parts. A prototype Mustang, A68-1001, was used for development trials and the first Australian production Mustang, A68-1, flew on 29 April 1945. The first 80 Mustang 20s (A68-1-80) were delivered with Packard Merlin V-1650-3 engines, under the CA-17 designation. A second contract called for 170 improved Mustangs, but only 120 were completed. Known as CA-18, the first 40 were built as Mustang 21s (A68-81-120) with Packard Merlin V-1650-7 engines. Mustangs A68-121 to -186 were fitted with modified Rolls Royce 66 and 70 Merlins Mk.66MUS and Mk.70MUS) and de Havilland propellers. The remaining CA-18s comprised 14 Mustang 22s (A68-187-200) with Packard Merlin V-1650-7 engines. (The Mk 22 was a photo reconnaissance variant.) A CA-21 contract for a further 250 Mustangs was cancelled and, in lieu of the remaining CA-18s and CA-21s, 298 lend-lease P-51Ds and Ks were taken on strength (A68-500-583 and A68-600-813). The Mustang saw long service with the Royal Australian Air Force (RAAF) and the Citizen Air Force (a reserve force). One CAC Mustang flies for the RAAF Museum, part of the RAAF, and is the last, and currently only, active Mustang in air force ownership.

Contract	Designation	Serial	Engine	Propeller
CA-17	Mk.20	A68-1 to 80	Packard V1650-3	Hamilton
CA-18	Mk.22	A68-81 to 94	Packard V1650-3	Hamilton
CA-18	Mk.21	A68-95 to 120	Packard V1650-7	Hamilton
CA-18	Mk.23	A68-121 to 186	Rolls Royce Mk.66MUS or Mk.70MUS*	de Havilland
CA-18	Mk.22	A68-187 to 200	Packard V1650-7	Hamilton

* These were ex MK. VIII Spitfire Merlin 66 and 70s modified to suit the CA-18 Mk.23 Mustang production as 66MUS and 70MUS respectively.

Commonwealth Aircraft Corporation Mustangs coming down the line at Fisherman's Bend in 1945. ***(RAAF Museum archive.)***

Later Mustangs

The P-51D was the main late mark, however there were further production models which did not supplant it. These were the P-51H and, for a different role, the P-82 Twin Mustang. In between were lightweight higher-performance versions the XP-51F, XP-51G and XP-51J. Only prototypes were built. The P-51H was a light-weight production version, which came too late for any action in World War II. Only 555 examples were built, and used by the USAF and the USANG during the late '40s and early '50s. Although this version looked similar to the P-51D/K it was a new design and only a few parts were interchangeable between the models. The engine used in this type was the Packard Merlin V-1650-9.

The P-82 Twin Mustang was a long-range version with two fuselages joined by a common centre section and tail. This, as the designation indicates, developed into a completely different type, even the fuselages and engines changing. Another distinct version seen today is the Cavalier Mustang, usually converted from a P-51D for civilian use by Trans-Florida Aviation (later renamed Cavalier Aircraft Corporation). Modifications included a second seat behind the pilot and sometimes tip tanks and a taller tail.

Mustang Survivors

There are more P-51D Mustangs airworthy at the time of writing than any other ex-military frontline type in history. This is in part due to the number built, wide postwar use, and the popular identification of the Mustang as 'THE' WWII fighter to the American public and elsewhere. There are about 150 Mustangs registered as airworthy, out of nearly 300 in preservation, the majority P-51D variants. There will probably be a Mustang close to most readers in Australasia, Europe and North America. For up to date information on Mustang dispositions, it is recommended to do an internet search the website www.mustangsmustangs.com is a good place to start. Although there is a significant drive towards authenticity (in incredible detail) in today's restorations, most surviving Mustangs are significantly different in finish and many details from how they would have appeared originally. This includes many national museum examples.

P-51H-1, 44-64164 in flight.
(Mike Jerram via Roger Wallsgrove)

Technical description

Wing.

Tapered, all-metal, two-spar wings. Dihedral angle 5°, laminar-flow wing section NAA-NACA, thickness ratio of 15.1 percent at the wing root at 39 percent of the chord, tip ratio 11.4 percent at the 50 percent chord line.

Wing sweep 0° at 25 percent of the chord. Both wings attached with bolts to the central rib in the airframe centreline. Wing upper surface in the cockpit area formed the cockpit floor. Each wing had 21 ribs. Removable wingtips, attached to wings with screws. Wing skin made of Alclad light alloy, riveted to ribs and longerons with countersunk rivets. Ailerons and flaps of metal structure hinged on rear spar, covered with light alloy skin. Ailerons of two-spar structure with 12 ribs, flaps of similar structure with 13 leading edge ribs and 15 central ribs.

Statically and dynamically balanced ailerons fitted with trimming tabs: port — adjustable, starboard — fixed. Ailerons operated mechanically with a system of tie rods, cranks and cables. Aileron deflection: 15° upwards and downwards. Hydraulically powered flaps deflected in the range of 0° - 50° at 10° intervals.

Fuselage.

Semi-monocoque fuselage made of duralumin (mainly Alclad — plated duralumin skin), divided into three sections joined with bolts. Front part housed the engine mount, central part the pilot's cockpit and engine radiator and the rear part the tail attachment points. Fuselage structure consisted of four main longerons drawn from duralumin plate, frames and additional longerons and was covered with stressed Alclad skin. Between front and central fuselage parts was the armour plate firewall separating the engine compartment from the cockpit.

P-51D Mustangs on the production line at the Inglewood factory. ***(Mike Jerram via Roger Wallsgrove)***

Front part of the fuselage was covered with four removable elements and three-part lower cowling. Engine cowling was attached to the structure with special quick-release locks. In the lower part of the cowling were three carburettor air intakes with air filters. The engine mount consisted of two box girders with auxiliary transverse struts. Both girders were joined with two U-shaped transverse frames. The entire unit was attached to the firewall with four bolts. Such a structure allowed quick removal of the engine from the airframe after removal of the engine cowling only.

The central fuselage was made of two halves joined at the fuselage centreline. Upper longerons of the central fuselage I-shaped at the front and T-shaped at the rear. Lower longerons also I-shaped at the front and C-shaped at the rear. Behind pilot's seat was a steel frame, which formed the turnover protection. Structurally, the central section consisted of eight parts joined with bolts and rivets.

The pilot's cockpit was fitted with a windshield made of armoured glass and a heating/cooling system. The front part of the windscreen made of five-layers of one inch thick armoured glass, sloped at 31°. Single-part, rear-sliding bubble-top canopy was made of Perspex and was reinforced in its lower part with a metal frame. In comparison with earlier versions the rear upper part of the fuselage was lowered to improve the pilot's rear view. The manually opened canopy was guided in special rails installed on both fuselage sides. It could be jettisoned in an emergency. Adjustable pilot's seat adapted for seat-type parachute. Adjustable rudder pedals. Behind the pilot's seat were two armoured plates protecting the pilot's head and back.

Semi-monocoque rear fuselage consisted of two longerons, three frames (walls), five auxiliary frames and a closing wall with tail attachment points.

Tail.

Tapered, two-spar cantilever horizontal tail unit covered with Alclad. Stabiliser fitted with removable tips facilitating installation and removal of elevators. Fabric-covered elevators deflected 30° upwards and 20° downwards. Later version had metal-covered elevators (P-51D-20NA and later versions). Elevators mass and aerodynamically balanced (with adjustable trim tabs). Two-spar fin covered with light alloy skin. Fin set 1° to port in relation to the airframe longitudinal centreline. From the P-51D-10NA version the aircraft was fitted with an additional dorsal fin. Earlier production aircraft were retrospectively fitted with it in the field. Rudder

P-51D-25-NA, serial 44-73186, N2-Y, 'Babs in Arms' of 383rd FS, 364th FG at 8th AF Station F-375, Honington, England, 21 May 1945. ***(USAF)***

was covered with mercerised cotton fabric and fitted with a trim tab. The elevator was operated with push-pull rods, bell cranks and cables. Elevator trim by cables and the rudder and rudder trim also by cables.

Landing gear.

Conventional landing gear with tail wheel. Single-leg main landing gear fitted with oleo-pneumatic shock absorbers, retractable in the direction of the longitudinal fuselage centreline. Retraction system powered hydraulically. Hydraulic disc brakes, controlled with rudder pedals. Main wheels of 68.5 cm diameter. Two-piece main wheel door. One piece was fastened to the wheel leg, the other one to the fuselage, covering the entire landing gear when fully retracted. Hydraulically retractable tail wheel with oleo-pneumatic shock absorbers. The tail wheel controlled by the rudder pedals via control cables. The tail wheel steering system could be disconnected during parking or taxiing through deflection of the control stick forward. The tail wheel is fully castoring with the stick forward. When the stick is back, movement, via rudder pedals, is limited to six degrees either side of fore & aft. Tail wheel bay fitted with two doors covering the bay when the tail wheel was fully retracted. Tail wheel diameter 32 cm.

Powerplant.

The aircraft was powered by a V-12, four-stroke, liquid-cooled, Packard V-1650-3, later V-1650-7 engine, or Rolls-Royce Merlin 68 licence-built by Packard Motor Car Co., Detroit.

Technical notes - Packard V-1650-7 engine (number made - 6325):

Cylinder banks angled at 60°, displacement 1,649 cu. in (27,029 cm^3), piston stroke 6 in (152.4 mm), cylinder bore 5.4 in (137.16 mm), compression ratio 6:1. The engine was fitted with reduction gear (0.479:1) and a two-stage, two-speed supercharger, which retained take-off power up to 25,590 ft (7,800 m). The supercharger was switched automatically to high blower between 15,700 and 19,700 ft (4,785 m & 6,000 m) – and was variable depending on rate of climb and descent, speed and the ram air at the carburetor intake.

Normal take-off power -1490 hp (1511 KM);

War emergency – 1720 hp (1744 KM)

Rated power 1315 hp (1333KM) (3000 rpm); maximum power 1720 hp (1744 KM) (3000 rpm)

Short-term, five-minute combat rating was 1,598 hp (1,620 KM) with boost pressure 2,065 hPa and 3,300 rpm.

Engine weight 1690 lb (766,57 kg), Length: 87.11 in. (2.21 m), Width: 29.97 in. (0.76 m), Height: 41.63 in. (1.057 m)

Equipment installed on the engine consisted of carburettor, two magnetos, propeller speed controller, fuel pump, oil pump, coolant pump, hydraulic system pump, generator, vacuum pump, starter and tachometer.

Engine control systems.

Merlin engines were fitted with a throttle lever mechanically connected to an an Automatic Boost Controller (made by Packard or Simmons), which controlled engine boost. The device kept constant engine boost pressure irrespective of flight conditions. On the rear part of the throttle quadrant was the fuel mixture control lever. The supercharger was controlled automatically, with the help of an aneroid connected to the electric system of the supercharger control unit. The engine used an electric starter.

Propeller.

Four-bladed Hydromatic-type Hamilton Standard 24D50-65 or -87 propeller. Propeller blades made of 6547-6, 6547A-6 or 6523A-24 aluminum alloy. Propeller diameter 11' 2" (3.40 m). The P-51K used a four-bladed, hydraulically-controlled A542S Unimatic propeller made by Aeroproducts. Propeller diameter 11' 1", blades H20-156P-23M5 made of steel. Both types were fitted with aluminium spinners.

*P-51D in England, an obviously "staged" photo, September 1944. (**USAF**)*

Propeller control system.

All P-51Ds were fitted with constant-speed propellers. The propeller pitch was controlled automatically depending on engine rotational speed.

Engine cooling system.

The aircraft was fitted with two independent cooling systems. The main cooling system had a capacity of 16.7 US gal (63 l) of coolant (30% solution of ethylene glycol in water). This included a header tank of 5.2 US gal (19.6 l) installed

Engine maintenance and an oil top up for a P-51D. Details of the engine panel frames are visible.

(Mike Jerram via Roger Wallsgrove)

on the front of the engine in the engine compartment. Both the main and after-cooler coolant system temperatures could be automatically or manually controlled via thermostat controlled electric actuators. The fuel mixture intercooler system was fitted with a separate radiator. Total volume of this system was 4.8 US gal (18 l) including the 0.5 US gal (1.9 l) header tank. Both the main and inter-cooler systems had individual engine driven coolant pumps.

Radiator tunnel outlet flaps were controlled automatically. The pilot could set one of four working modes: automated, open, closed, control off.

Engine Oil system.

The engine oil system had a total capacity of 21 US Gal (79.4 l). The engine oil tank was mounted on the forward face of the main firewall between the cockpit and engine compartment, and had a capacity of 12.5 US gal (47.3 l) plus 1 US gal air space for expansion. The oil cooler was installed in the tunnel under the fuselage. Oil temperature was controlled automatically by a thermostatically controlled actuator and could be set in one of four modes the same as the coolant actuator. The oil system limited the time of inverted flight to ten seconds.

Fuel system.

Fuel system consisted of two 92 US gal (348 1) tanks installed in the wing roots between spars and an additional 85 US gal (321 l) tank in the fuselage just behind the pilot's seat.

The aircraft could carry two additional jettisonable underwing tanks. In the cockpit was a lever for mechanical jettisoning of underwing tanks in the case of failure of the electric release system. Recommended fuel octane rating 100/130. Floatless pressure injection carburettor, fed by a 600 gallon per hour engine driven fuel pump.

P-51D-25-NA, 44-72719, N2•D, 'Constance' of 364th FG, 67th FW, 8th AF, personal aircraft of Lt. Col. G. F. Ceullers, 8th AF Station F-375, Honington, England, 23 April 1945. (USAF)

Flight instruments.

Airspeed indicator, remote indicating compass, directional gyro, clock, vertical speed indicator, accelerometer and altimeter, artificial horizon, turn & bank indicator.

Engine control instruments.

Manifold pressure (boost) gauge, coolant temperature gauge, rpm gauge, carburettor air inlet temperature gauge, oil temperature gauge and fuel pressure gauge.

Other instruments.

Oxygen pressure gauge, hydraulic pressure gauge, vacuum guage and ammeter.

Electrical system.

24 volt, supplied from 28 volt, 100-Ampere generator driven by the engine. If the generator voltage fell below 26.5V, the system was supplied from a 24 volt battery of 34 Ah capacity. In earlier versions the battery was installed in the bay just behind pilot's seat armour, in later version (D/K) the battery was moved to the engine compartment. Additionally, the aircraft was fitted with an 26 V, 400 Hz alternator supplying power to the remote

Wartime photo of P-51D instrument panel. K-14A gunsight is visible. (USAF)

indicating compass. The electrical system included the supercharger control system, instrumentation, oil cooler and coolant radiator flap control system, landing gear warning system, engine starter, fuel boost pumps, machine gun triggers and gun sight, radio power supply, pitot heat and lighting. External lights included navigation lights and landing lights installed in the landing gear wells.

Oxygen system.

The oxygen system consisted of two D-2 and two F-2 bottles and an AN6004 (earlier production batches) or A-12 controller.

Equipment.

Above the instrument panel was N-9 reflector gunsight or K-14 gyro-computing gunsight. Machine gun and bomb rack triggers were located on the control stick.

Radio equipment.

Radio equipment consisted of one transmitter and three receivers of SCR-522, SCR-515, SCR-535 or SCR-695 type. Radio equipment was accommodated in fuselage compartments behind the cockpit.

Later versions (P-51D-25) were fitted with AN/ARC-3 transceiver, AN/ARA-8 direction finder/homing adapter and AN/APX-6 IFF transponder.

Armament.

P-51D/Ks were armed with three 0.5 in (12.7 mm) Browning M2 machine guns fitted with J-l or J-4 gun heaters. Inboard guns had initially 500 and later 400 rounds per gun, central and outboard guns had 280 rpg.

P-51D-15-NA Mustang, 44-14886, during tests with tube rocket launchers. (USAF)

P-51D/K serial batches:

Inglewood-built P-51Ds			
44-13253/14052	P-51D-5-NA Mustang	c/n 109-26886/27685	800
44-14053/14852	P-51D-10-NA Mustang	c/n 109-27686/28485	800
44-14853/15752	P-51D-15-NA Mustang	c/n 109-28486/28885, 35536/36035	900
44-63160/64159	P-51D-20-NA Mustang	c/n 122-30806/31885	1000
44-72027/72626	P-51D-20-NA Mustang	c/n 122-31886/31985,38586/39085	600
44-72627/74226	P-51D-25-NA Mustang	c/n 122-39086/40085, 40167/40766	1600
44-74227/75026	P-51D-30-NA Mustang	c/n 122-40767/41566	800

Dallas-built P-51Ds			
44-11153/11352	P-51D-5-NT Mustang	c/n 111-29286/29485	200
44-12853/13252	P-51D-20-NT Mustang	c/n 111-36136/36535	400
44-84390/84989	P-51D-25-NT Mustang	c/n 124-44246/44845	600
45-11343/11542	P-51D-25-NT Mustang	c/n 124-48096/48295	200
45-11543/11742	P-51D-30-NT Mustang	c/n 124-48296/48495	200

total of 8100 P-51Ds.

Serials of the P-51K:			
44-11353/11552	P-51K-1-NT Mustang	c/n 111-29486/29685	200
44-11553/11952	P-51K-5-NT Mustang	c/n 111-29686/30085	400
44-11953/12552	P-51K-10-NT Mustang	c/n 111-30086/30685	600
44-12553/12852	P-51K-15-NT Mustang	c/n 111-30686/30885, 111-36036/36135	300

total of 1500 P-51Ks.

Swedish P-51D, (J 26), 'B' on the skies during tests.
(Archive Svensk Flyghitorisk Förening)

P-51D-5-NA Mustang specification

Fuselage length: 32 ft 3 in (9.84 m)
Wing span: 37 ft 0 in (11.27 m)
Wing aspect ratio: 4.46
Wing incidence: approx 1°
Wing dihedral angle (at 25% line): 5°
Wing sweepback angle (leading edge): 3° 3' 32"
Tailplane span: 13 ft 21/8 in (3.83 m)
Total wing area: 233.19 sq ft (21.66 m^2)
Total aileron area: 12.64 sq ft (1.17 m^2)
Total flap area: 32.60 sq ft (3.03 m^2)
Total horizontal tail area: 27.85 sq ft (2.59 m^2)
Total elevator area: 13.05 sq ft (1.21 m^2)
Fin area: 8.83 sq ft (0.82 m^2)
Rudder area: 10.25 sq ft (0.95 m^2)
Overall height: 13 ft 8 in (4.16 m) (taxiing attitude, statically loaded)
Landing gear track: 11 ft 10 in (3.61 m)
Maximum wing loading: 49.7 lb/sq ft (242.9 kg/m^2)

Engine: One Packard-built Merlin V-1650-7 liquid-cooled 12-cylinder Vee inline piston engine with two-speed two-stage supercharger, driving an 11 ft 2-in (3.40-m) diameter Hamilton Standard constant-speed hydromatic four-bladed propeller

Take-off rating: 1,450 hp (1,094 kW)
War emergency ratings: 1,695 hp (1,264 kW) at 10,300 ft (3,139 m) and 1,390 hp (1,036 kW) at 24,000 ft (7,315 m)
Military ratings: 1,550 hp (1,156 kW) at 13,000 ft (3,962 m) and 1,260 hp (940 kW) at 26,500 ft (8,077 m)
Continuous ratings: 1,150 hp (858 kW) at 17,000 ft (5,182 m) and 980 hp (731 kW) at 29,000 ft (8,839 m)
Propeller pitch range: 23° - 65°

Weights.
Empty operating: 7,125 lb (3,232 kg)
Basic: 7,635 lb (3,466 kg)
Combat weight (clean): 10,100 lb (4,582 kg)
Maximum take-off: 11,600 lb (5,262 kg) with two 108-US gal (409-litre) drop tanks

Fuel and load.
Total internal fuel: 269 US gal (1018 litres), comprising 184 US gal (696 litres) in self-sealing wing fuel cells, plus 85 US gal (322 litres) in self-sealing fuselage tank.
External fuel: provision for two 75 US gal (284-litre), 110 US gal (416-litre) or 108 US gal (409 litre) fuel tanks.
Maximum weapon load: 2,000 lb (908 kg)

Performance

Maximum level speeds: (clean, no racks fitted) 395 mph (636 km/h) at 5,000 ft (1,524 m), 413 mph (665 km/h) at 15,000 ft (4,572 m), 437 mph (703 km/h) at 25,000 ft (7,620 m) and 433 mph (697 km/h) at 30,000 ft (9,144 m)
Maximum speed below 9,000 ft: 505 mph (812 km/h) With droptanks: 400 mph (643 km/h)
Maximum cruising speed: 362 mph (583 km/h)
Rate of climb: 3,475 ft (1,059 m) per minute at 5,000 ft (1,524 m)
Service ceiling: 41,900 ft (12,771 m)
Time to climb: 20,000 ft (6,096 m) in 7 minutes 20 seconds, 30,000 ft (9,144 m) in 12 minutes 36 seconds
Landing speed: 100 mph (161 km/h)

Armament

Fixed: six wing-mounted 0.50-in (12.7-mm) Colt-Browning M2 machine guns, with a total of 1,880 rounds, comprising 400 rounds for each inboard gun and 270 rounds each for the outboard pairs

External stores: two underwing hardpoints for two 500 lb (227-kg) or 1,000 lb (454 kg) free-fall general-purpose bombs, or bazooka-type tubes for six 4.5-in (114-mm) M-8 explosive rockets or (from P-51D-25-NA) six 5 in (127 mm) high-velocity aircraft rockets (HVARs) carried on zero-length launchers with tanks or bombs, or 10 HVARS without tanks or bombs.

Version	Spec Range (Miles/MPH/ALT)		Fuel (US Gal)		Bombs (lb)		Weight (lb)	
P-51D-NA (-1 to –30) P-51D-NT (-5, -20, -25) Engine V-1650-3 or –7 With 85 gallon fuselage tank	Ferry	2300/245/10000	Max	489	None	-	Ferry	11600
	Normal	950/362/25000	Built-in	269	Normal	1000	Normal	11100
	Design	400/370/25000	Design	105	Design	-	Design	8600
P-51K-NT (-1 to -15) Engine V-1650-7 With 85 gallon fuselage tank	Ferry	2300/245/10000	Max	489	None	-	Ferry	11600
	Normal	950/362/25000	Built-in	269	Normal	1000	Normal	11100
	Design	400/370/25000	Design	105	Design	-	Design	8600

Commonwealth Aircraft Corporation Mustang production in full swing at Fisherman's Bend, Melbourne, Victoria, Australia in 1945.

(RAAF Museum Archive)

Swedish P-51D, (J 26), 'B', (16). The aircraft in this photo features a canopy with a different shape (see page 18 for more details).

(Archive Svensk Flyghitorisk Förening)

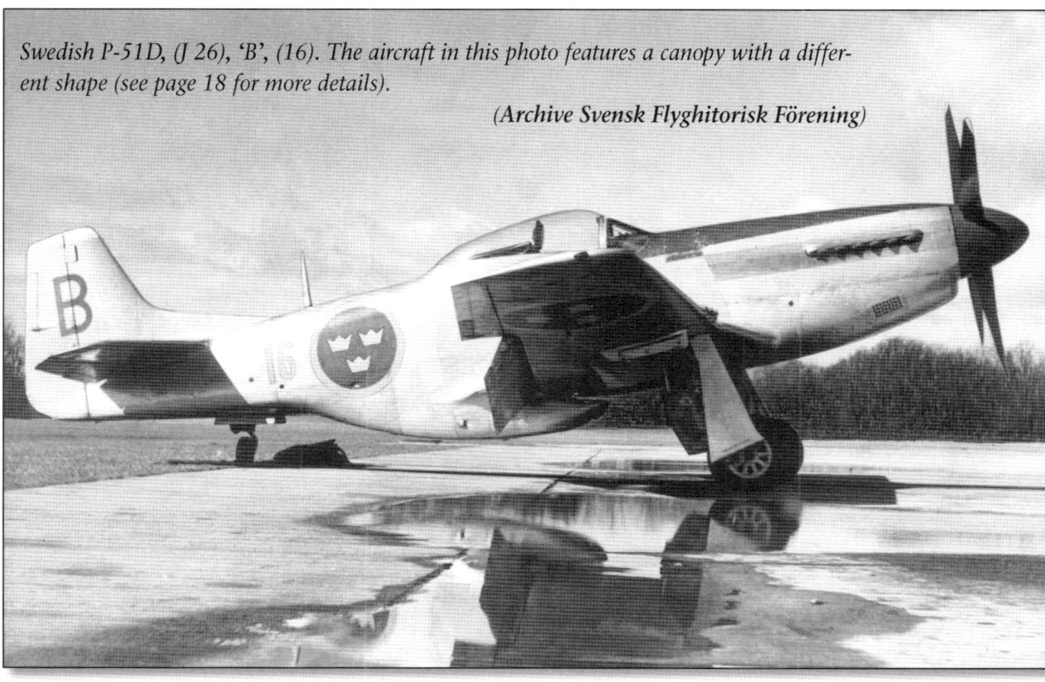

The CAC Flightline at Fisherman's Bend, with a Mustang 22 (the camera port visible just aft of the roundel) being prepared for flight.

(RAAF Museum archive)

3 Squadron RAAF P-40s (a 450 Squadron example in the background) were replaced by North American built Mustang Mk.IV fighters in Italy. The 'Southern Cross' tail marking of white stars on a pale blue background is visible.

(RAAF Museum archive)

Mustang Walkround: General views

A preserved CAC-built Mustang representing an American-built, RAAF operated example. The RAAF Museum's A68-170 (VH-SVU) represents A68-750 in Japanese occupation force colours.

(James Kightly)

Lots of detail here of P-51D-30NA 'Happy Jack's Go Buggy' 44-74452 (N74190) as recently restored to the highest standard by Mike Vanboncouer's team at Midwest Aero Restorations for Bruce Winter. As well as picking up numerous trophies, this Mustang is generally held to be the most authentically restored example flying, and offers numerous details focussed on in the following sections. Note here the overall appearance, sheens and reflections of the aircraft.

(Midwest Aero Restorations)

Showing the 'plain' side of Happy Jack's Go Buggy, again the sheens of the natural metal and Olive Drab are evident. Note also the complex colour effect and extent of the exhaust trail. In wartime both white and black soots could be seen here as well depending on how the engine was being used.

(Midwest Aero Restorations)

P-51D-20-NA serial 44-72483, painted as P-51D-20-NA, serial 44-63507, SX•B, 'Double Trouble Two', current registration N51EA.

(Stratus)

Inspection and Access Panels.

1. Rudder Lower Hinge Access Fairing
2. Vertical Stabiliser Aft Right-hand Fairing
3. Vertical Słabilizer Forward Fairing
4. Fuselage to Horizonfal Stabiliser Fairing
5. Aft Wing to Fuselage Fairing
6. Oxygen Filler Valve Access Door
7. Hydraulic Reservoir Access Cover
8. Oxygen Lines and Instruments
9. Engine Access Upper Cowlings
10. Engine Access Side Cowlings
11. Engine Crank Access Hole
12. Engine Heating Access Door
13. Engine Access Lower Forward Cowling
14. Engine Access Lower Intermediate Cowling
15. Engine Access Lower Aft Cowling
16. Wing to Fuselage Forward Fairing
17. Wing to Fuselage Intermediate Fairing
18. Main Landing Gear Pivot Shaft Access Door
19. Running Light Access
20. Ammunition Bay Access Door
21. Gun Bay Access Door
22. Aileron Cable Turnbuckle Inspection Cover
23. Wing Fuel Tank Filler Cap
24. Front Scoop Attachment Bolt Access
25. Oil Radiator Line Access Door
26. Aftercooler Line Hose Access
27. External Power Pług Access Cover
28. Radiator Cover Bolts Access Door
29. Radiator Cover Attachment Bolts Access Door
30. Radiator Cover Assembly
31. Tail Gear Down-lock Access Door
32. Tail Gear Up-latch Access Door
33. Elevator Trim Tab Actuating Drum Access Door
34. Coolant Tank Filler Neck Access Door
35. Aftercooler Tank Access Door
36. Oil Tank Filler Neck Access Door
37. Engine Controls and Instrument Access Cover
38. Rudder Trim Tab Cable Rollers Access Door
39. Rudder Trim Tab Actuating Cable Drum Access Door
40. Vertical Stabiliser Aft Left-hand Fairing
41. Rudder Bellcrank Access Door
42. Tail Gear Up-latch and Actuating Strut Access Door

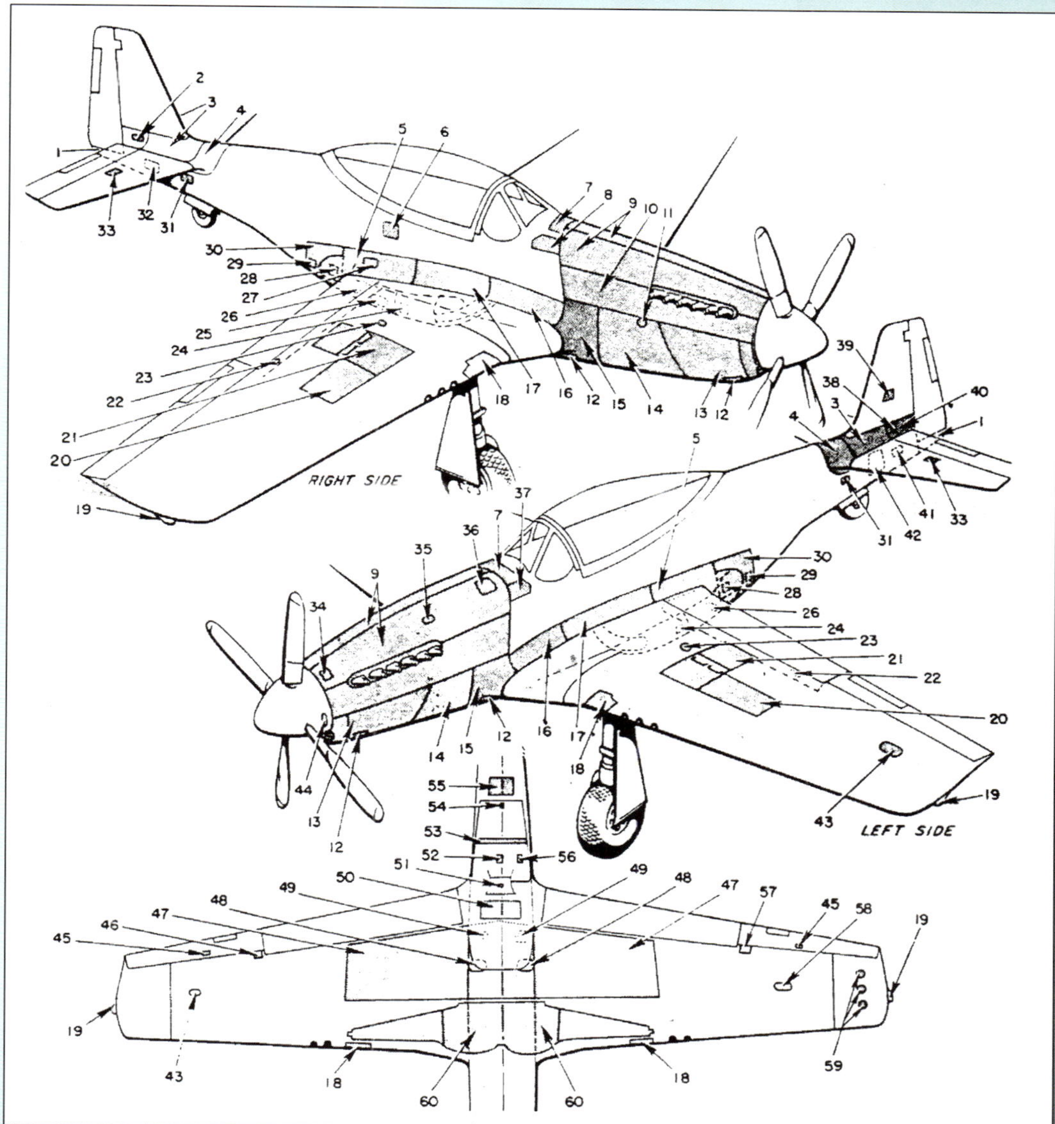

43. Remote-reading Compass Access Door
44. Propeller Governor Access Door
45. Aileron Center Hinge Access Door
46. Aileron Trim Tab Actuating Drum Access Door
47. Fuel Tank Doors
48. Euel Booster Pump Access Doors
49. Fuel Tank Drain Cock Access
50. Oil Radiator Access Door
51. Oil Radiator Rear Scoop Actuating Rod Access Plate
52. Coolant Drain Access Door
53. Rear Scoop Hinge Access Door
54. Rear Scoop Actuating Rod Access Plate
55. Control Cable and Oxygen Cylinder Access Door
56. Aftercooler Drain Access Door
57. Aileron Boost Tab Actuating Fitting Door
58. Remote Contactor Mast Access Door
59. Recognition Lights and Access
60. Wheel Well Fairing Doors

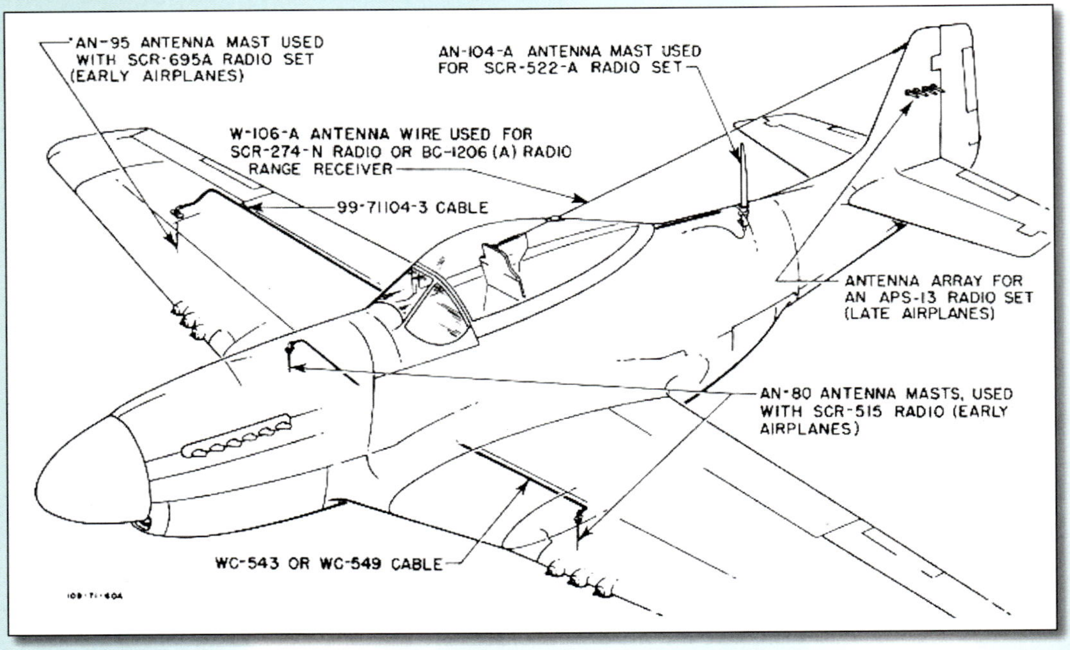

Above: *P-51D aerials.* ***(Drawing from Technical Manual)***
Below: *P-51D-25NA (44-73339), representing serial 44-74008, when owned by David Gilmour of the rock group Pink Floyd, and named after the song 'Comfortably Numb'.* ***(Dariusz Karnas Coll.)***

Above: *P-51D-5NA, serial 44-13704, 'Ferocious Frankie'.* ***(Stratus)***
Below: *P-51K-1-NT, 44-12472, in French colours as 'Annemasse'.* ***(James Kightly)***

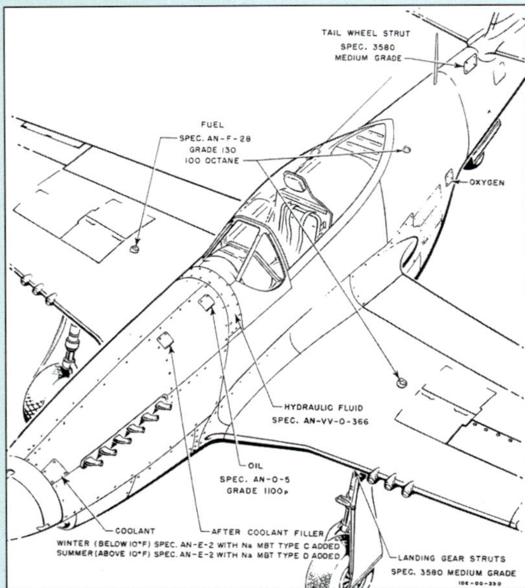

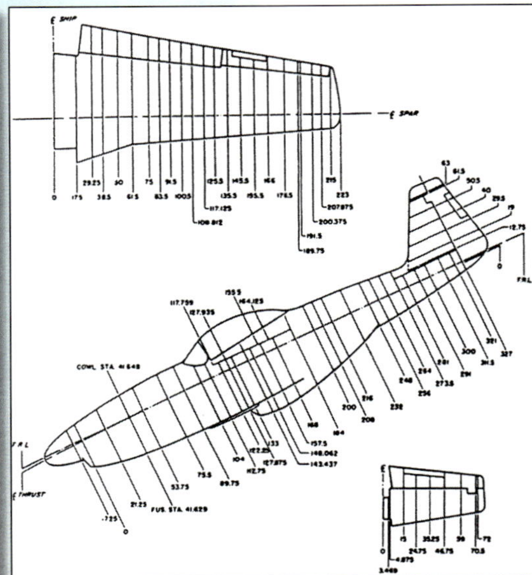

Above left: *P-51D servicing diagram.* **Above right:** *P-51 Stations Diagram. Both from Technical Manual.* **Below:** *Early morning wake-up call for the Mustangs on the ramp. Rickenbacker Airport, Columbus Ohio, 2007 at the second 'Gathering of Mustangs & Legends'.* ***(Airshow Traveler)***

Built as P-51D-30-NA, serial 44-74446, in markings of P-51D-5-NA, serial 44-13498, '11', personal aircraft of Hershel 'Herky' Green, 319th FS, 325th FG, 15th AF. Registration NL1451D.

*(**Airshow Traveler**)*

Below: *P-51D-30-NA, serial 44-74409 at the RAF Museum, Hendon, painted as 44-13317, VF•B, originally flown by Donald Emerson. The nose painted with a 'Donald Duck' artwork as seen on Emerson's original P51D.*

*(**Stratus**)*

Above: *This shot shows the take-off configuration of the P-51D type. CAC Mustang VH-JUC has the landing light deployed (with the gear) clamshell doors closed and flaps up. This aircraft has a non-original second 'jump-seat' fitted, from where the passenger is filming.*

(James Kightly)

Below: *The same Mustang, showing the landing configuration, with the flaps partly deployed*

(James Kightly)

Two photos of a Mustang painted as P-51D-20-NA, serial 44-72218, WZ•I, 'Big Beautiful Doll'. Built as CA-18 Mk 22, serial A68-192. Registered as G-HAEC. **(Dariusz Karnas)**

Above: *CAC18 Mk.22 Mustang A68-192 (G-HAEC) showing the wing plan form and RAAF colours at Duxford.*
Below: *P-51D Mustang G-CBNM in 78th FG colours as 'Twilight Tear' presents a very authentic-looking patina at the 100 Years of Flight display at the Royal International Air Tattoo in 2003.* (**Both James Kightly**)

Port side of the forward fuselage of the Scandinavian Historic Flight's Mustang painted as Bud Anderson's 'Old Crow'. ***(James Kightly)***

As 'Happy Jack's Go Buggy' breaks away from the camera aircraft, numerous details can be made out. The complex patterning around the radiator intake and the different natural metals of the clamshell gear doors are one area where the construction technique left the evidence in the natural metal finish of the day. The scheme is that of ace Jack Ilfrey, of the 79th fighter squadron, 20th Fighter Group, of the 8th Air Force. ***(Midwest Aero Restorations)***

This shot, almost a profile, shows the sheen and path of the exhaust stain, the flaps slightly deployed to maintain control at a lower speed to stay with the camera aircraft, and the slightly open radiator outlet. Also worth noting is the impression of the 'cuffed' propeller, and the position and appearance of the pilot's head and equipment wearing period garb. This could be a 1945 photograph. ***(Midwest Aero Restorations)***

Above: A great diorama opportunity, this shows a Mustang fuselage being mated to its wing. Note the finishes of the surfaces – natural metal and coated on the wing, and the canopy being covered with a opaque film, the windscreen with masking. The clipboards on the rear fuselage are also of interest. **(via James Kightly)**

Below: This photograph shows Mustangs intended for four different operators after test flights at Inglewood in 1945. In the left foreground is a Mustang for the RAAF, indicated by the wing roundel, with another further back revealed by its fin flash. In front of that one is a Mustang with a Dutch Netherlands East Indies Air Force (NEIAF) fuselage marking. On the right hand side, there is a Mustang Mk.IV for the RAF, KM703 being refuelled. These aircraft were from the 44-844xx serial block, KM703 being 44-84468. **(James Kightly Collection)**

Fuselage

P-51D-20-NA, serial 44-72560, "603" of 462nd FS, 506th FG, 20th AF, Iwo Jima. Note the double antennae behind the cockpit. . These worked with the AN/ARA-8 radio homing units, nicknamed 'Uncle Dog' which were used to receive a special homing signal sent from Iwo Jima to guide the pilots home from their very long range (VLR) missions to Japan. ***(USAF)***

Starboard side of CA-18 Mk 22, serial A68-192, in RAAF colours. ***(James Kightly)***

Top Right: The starboard side of the forward fuselage of G-HAEC, in Colonel John Landers' colours, with the wing fillet visible.
(James Kightly)

Middle: Another preserved CAC-built Mustang representing an American-built but RAAF operated example. Judy Pay and Richard Hourigan's VH-JUC in wartime Italian campaign colours. In almost exact profile, seen on take off, note the flaps are up, but the radiator door is open.
(James Kightly)

Right: Port side of the fuselage just behind the cockpit showing partial D-Day stripes.
(Dariusz Karnas Archive)

Below: Accurately recreated stencils on the rear fuselage of 'Happy Jack's Go Buggy'.
(Steve Atkin)

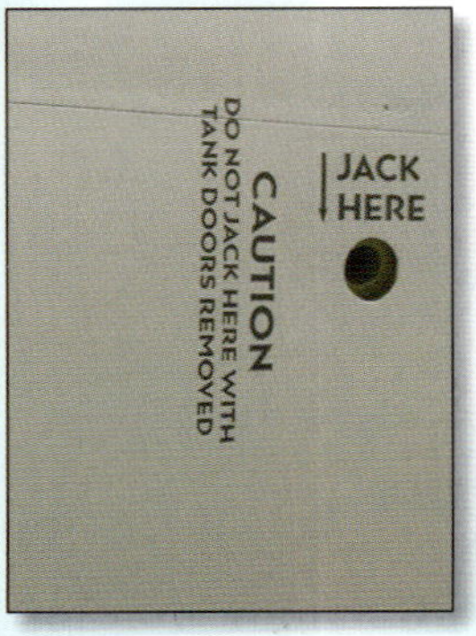

Carefully recreated details on the Midwest Aero Restorations Mustang rebuild of P-51D-30NA 44-74452 (N74190) 'Happy Jack's Go Buggy'.
Top: *Stencil and period style marks around the access panels have been recreated (see page 57).*

The detail extends even to the interior fittings, the colours and look of the piping, wiring and finish.

In contrast, a very high shine to the finish (still with accurate stencil markings) have been applied to 'Daddy's Girl'.
(All Steve Atkin)

A view of the radiator intake on VH-JUC. This is lower (further away from the fuselage) than the earliest Mustangs, and contains the oil and engine radiators, the oil cooler being below.

(James Kightly)

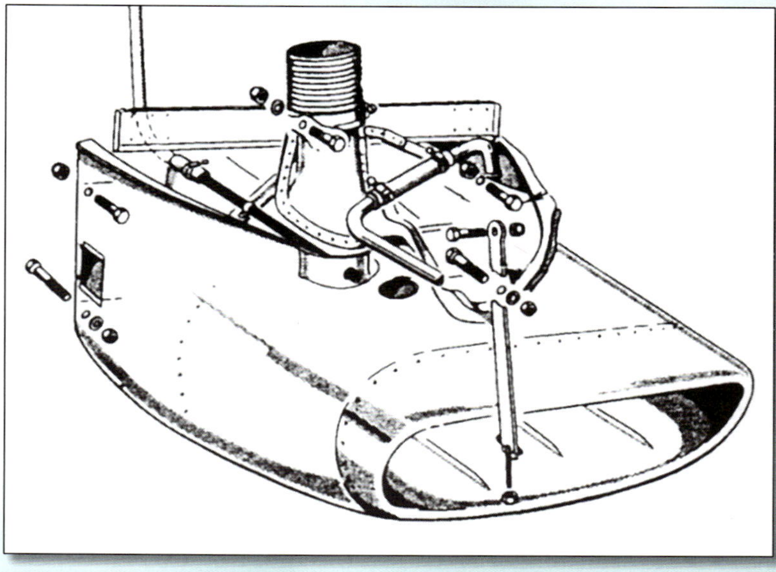

Drawing from Technical Manual showing radiator mounting system.

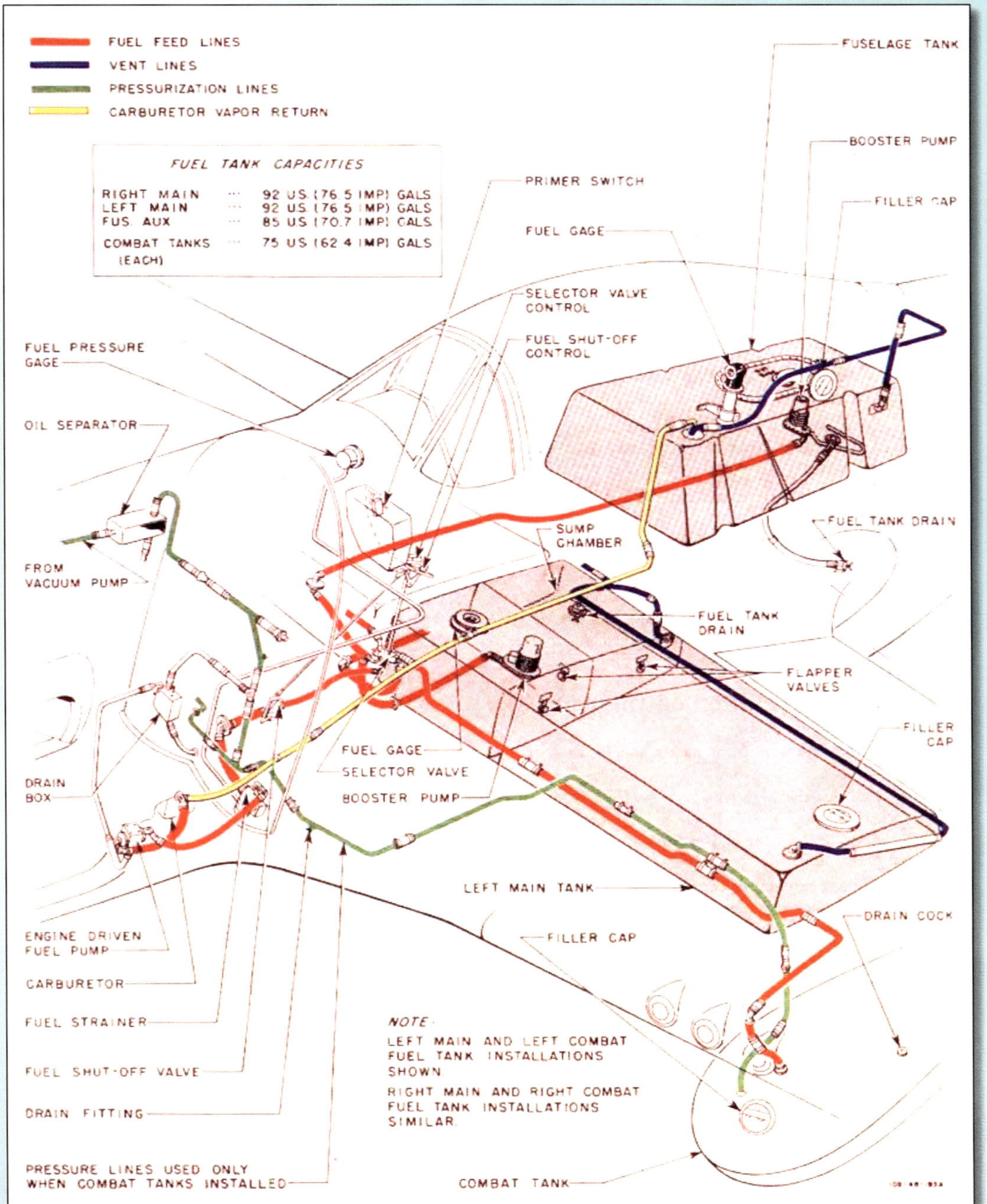

P-51D fuel system drawing from Pilot's Manual.

The rear fuselage scheme and stencil as seen on Commonwealth disruptive-camouflaged Mustangs, here, VH-JUC. The extensive stencils are visible, and the visible wooden base to the fuselage aerial can be seen.

(James Kightly)

This is a closer view showing the stencils, including the reference to the 'DATA CASE' shown on page 54.

(James Kightly)

Above: *Port side of the fuselage. Note that radiator exhaust flaps are open. Also the landing flaps are in the lowered position as the hydraulic pressure has bled off. This Mustang belongs to Jerry Yagen's Fighter Factory collection at his new Military Aviation Museum at Virginia Beach, USA.*

Below: *Starboard side of the radiator, all panel lines are clearly visible.*

*(**All Stratus**)*

Looking up and into the rear fuselage from the radiator position, of 'Happy Jack's Go Buggy' showing the oxygen tanks and data case, all in the correct colours and details. Note also the control cables and their markings and tags shown.
(Midwest Aero Restorations)

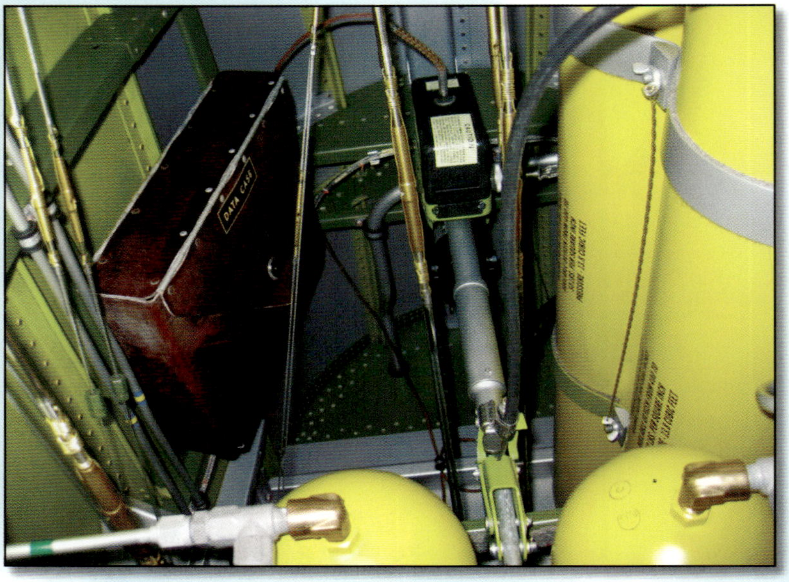

Another view looking in the same direction, but from higher up. The different interior finishes are evident, as are the stencils and placards on the tanks and the radiator outlet jack.
(Midwest Aero Restorations)

Above & Left: *Three photos of the radiator outlet with flap in the open position on the RAF Museum's Mustang.*

Bottom, right: *Main fuel tank filler cap and "Ground Here" jack.*

(All Stratus)

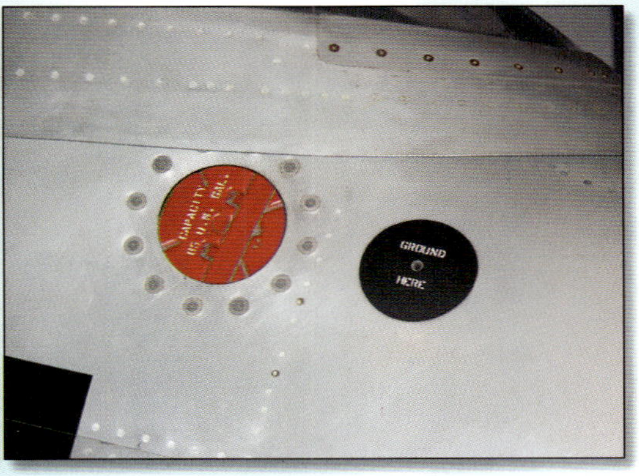

Right: *Mustang nose as seen from below. The propeller is not at a flightworthy pitch angle.*

Below: *Central, starboard part of the fuselage.*

Above, right: *Starboard side of the rear part of the radiator.*

Right: *Radiator outlet, flap in open position.*
(All Stratus)

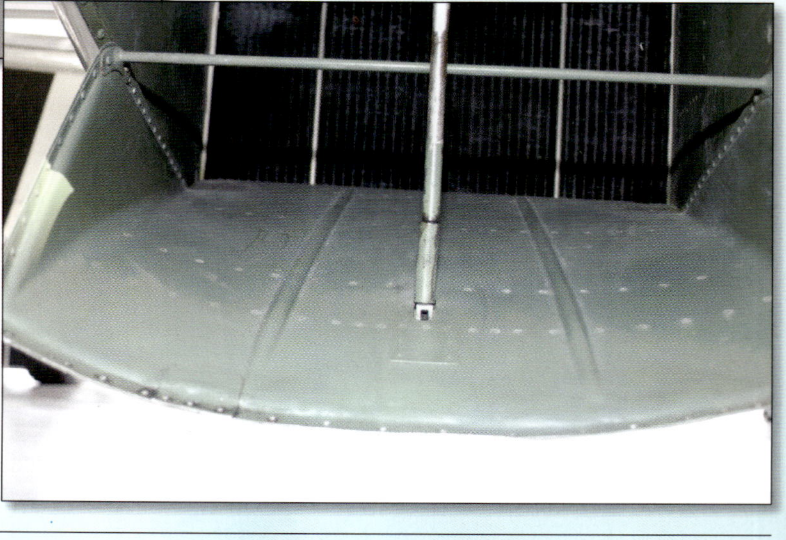

Wing

This underside view of 'Happy Jack's Go Buggy' shows the variegated finish that would have appeared on wartime Mustangs. Mike VadeBonCoeur explains "Looking at factory photos you can see where that metal was etched with acid, because when you do the aluminum spot welding process, the metal has to be perfectly clean and one of the ways they did that was with an acid etch cleaner. So certain areas, for instance the front scoop, and some of the areas on the aft door back, they just brushed acid on, and then put the two pieces together and did the spot welding."

The rear centre section has a number of reddish lines visible as well. Mike again: "Metal manufacturers such as Alcoa and Reynolds use what are called 'water marks' to identify materials. The code usually specifies the alloy, temper and thickness and of course the manufacturer. It was done with a red dye and when a panel was to be primed with yellow chromate, the red would bleed through and you could see the marks. Throughout the aircraft, original (not modern) style is something we tried to simulate. We replicated three different fonts and styles that we found on the Mustangs."

(Midwest Aero Restorations)

Different wing treatments on preserved Mustangs. Below, the Mustang in the Smithsonian Museum, Washington DC (P-51D-30NA, 44-74939, 'Willit Run') shows a plain metal finish, while the Mustang in the RAF Museum, 44-74409, has a painted finish. P-51s left the factory with a dull silver paint finish to the wings (this was to seal the application of filler and primer to the leading edges in order to ensure a perfectly smooth aerodynamic finish needed for the laminar flow design).

(All Stratus)

Above: *The laminar flow wing section is clear here, as is the original wingtip navigation and modern formation light configuration.*
Below: *Looking from the wingtip on the RAAF Museum's airworthy Mustang shows the laminar-flow airfoil section and the slightly concave upper flap surface.*

(James Kightly)

Two examples of the recognition lights on the underside of the starboard wing. Seen on the RAF Museum's Mustangs at Cosford and Hendon.

Details of of the starboard aileron and landing flap.
(All Stratus)

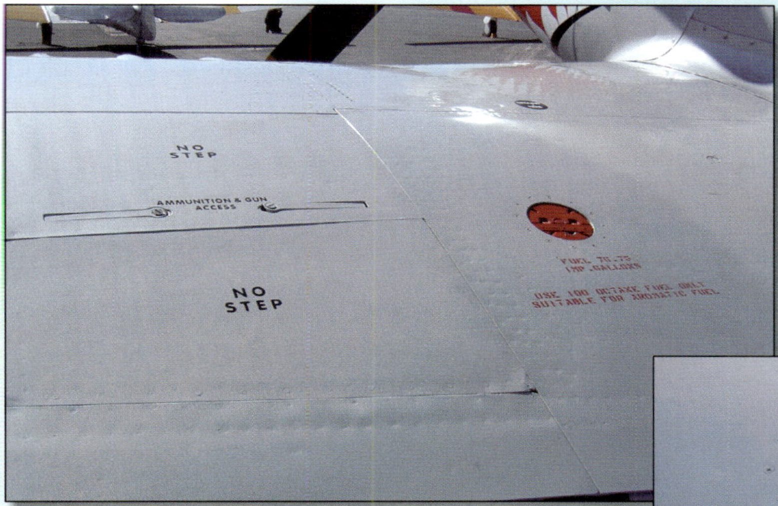

The fuel filler cap and gun bay cover on the RAAF Museum's CAC-built example.
(James Kightly)

Below: *The correct stenciling shown on Happy Jack's Go Buggy'.*
(Steve Atkin)

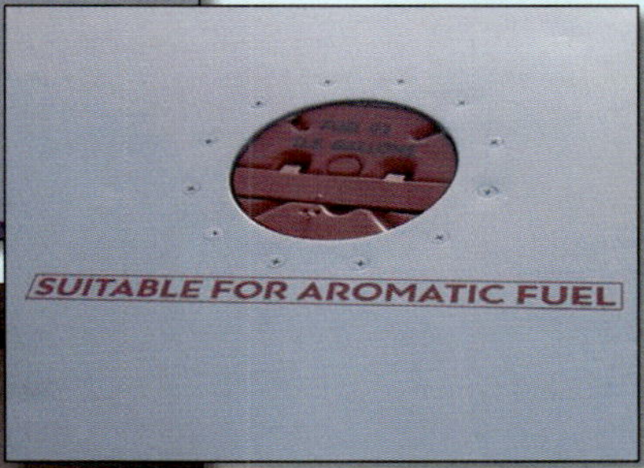

Left: *The port aileron and aileron tab details.*
(Stratus)

Starboard, central part of the Mustang wing. Wing fuel tank filler and machine gun panels are visible.
(Stratus)

Two photos of pitot head under the starboard wing. ***(All Stratus)***

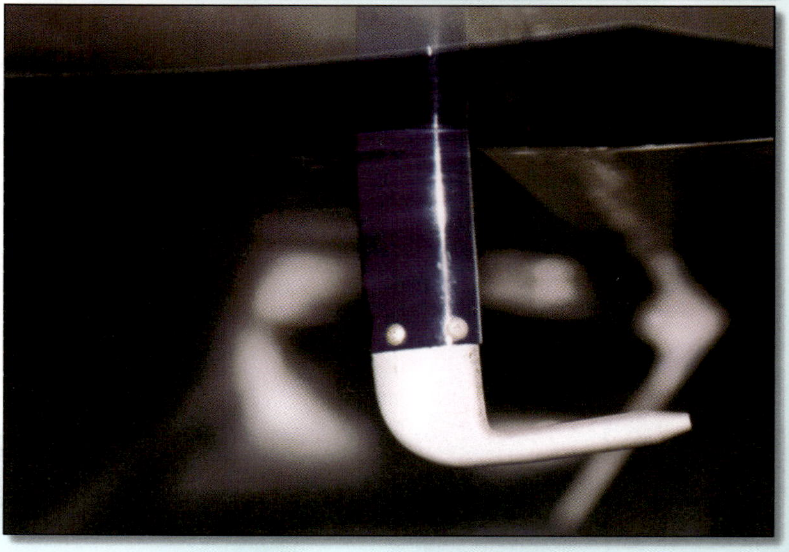

Close-up shot of the aileron tab actuator. (**Stratus**)

The inner aileron attachment and flap hinge line. (**James Kightly**)

Camera gun on the port wing. (**Stratus**)

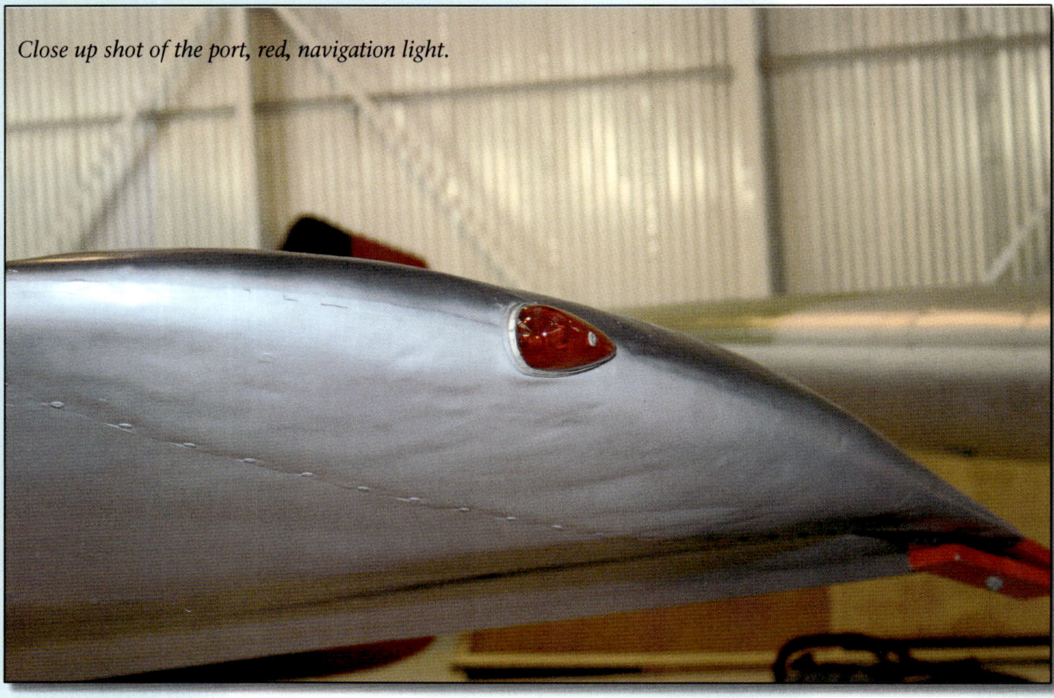

Close up shot of the port, red, navigation light.

Port landing flap fully extended.
(All Stratus)

Starboard flap, also in landing position.
(Stratus)

Below: *Landing flap actuator.* **(Stratus)**
Bottom, left: *The flap index marking graduations here show evidence of wear.* **(James Kightly)**

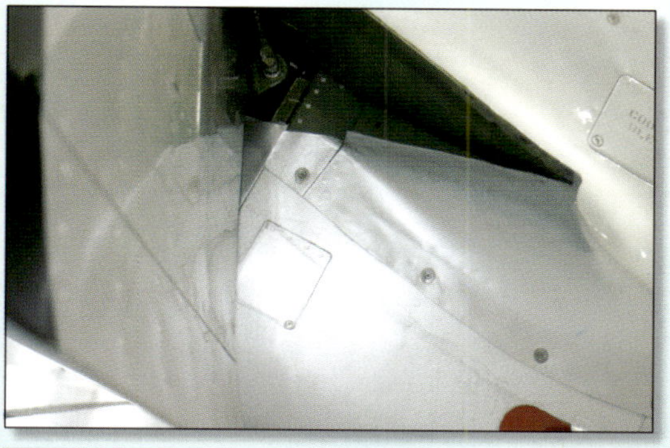

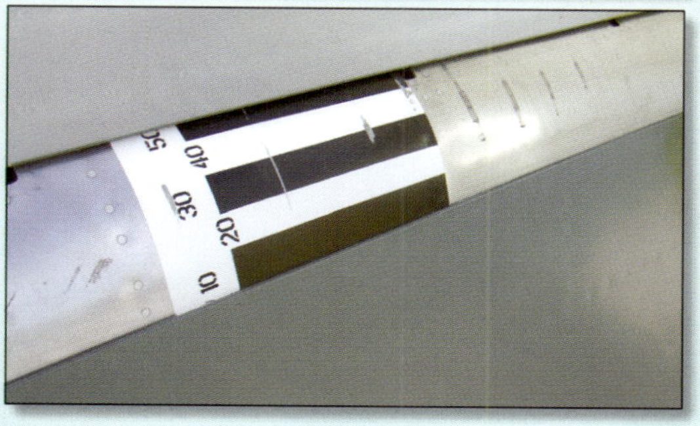

Flap position indicator.
(Stratus)

Engine

NORTH AMERICAN AVIATION, INC.
PHOTOGRAPHIC DEPARTMENT
INGLEWOOD CALIFORNIA

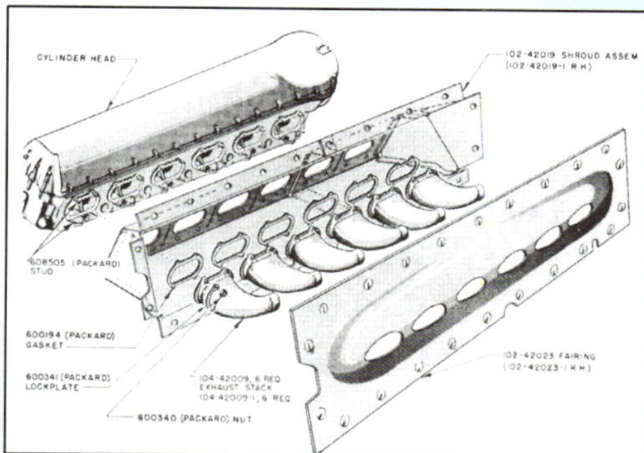

Details of the exhaust. Drawing from Technical Manual

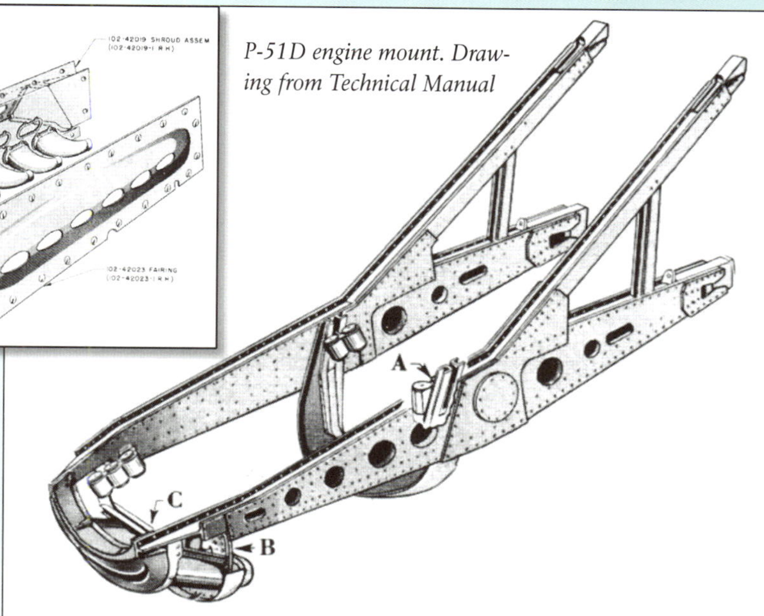

P-51D engine mount. Drawing from Technical Manual

Cowling supports. Drawing from Technical Manual.

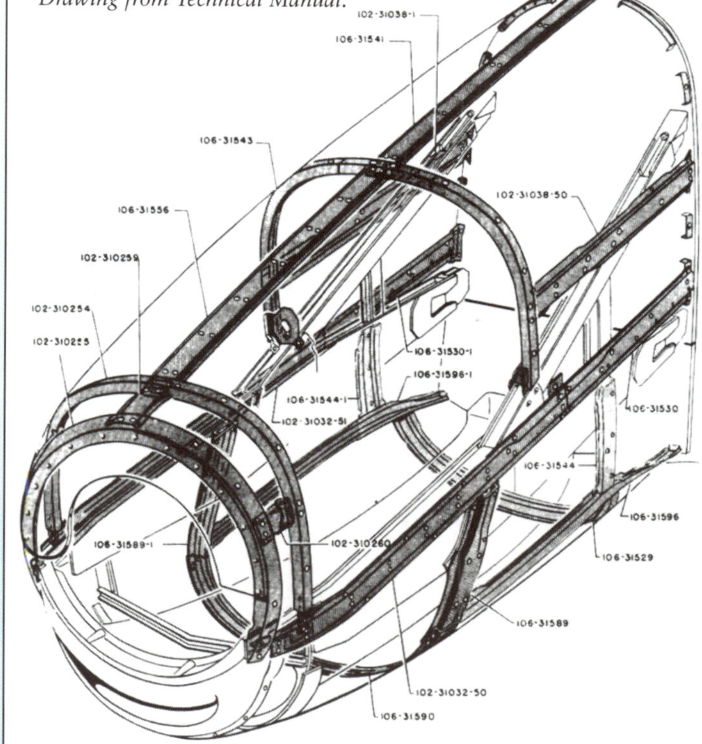

Opposite page top: *Adjusting the Magneto timing. All panels are removed.*

(Mike Jerram via Roger Wallsgrove).

Opposite page bottom: *Australian used Packard Merlin engines built up as units to the Mustang production at Fisherman's Bend, Melbourne. It is rare to see the Mustang engine unit as a single separate item.*

(CAC via James Kightly)

*Details of the engine on a restored aircraft. (**Stratus**)*

The nose of 'Happy Jack's Go Buggy' showing the numerous markings. The lacquer covered data panel is clear, with the cross indicating an aircraft with the large long-range fuselage tank fitted. Midwest Aero tinted the urethane slightly yellowish brown to replicate the in-service aging lacquer.

(James P Church)

With the central side panel removed, some of the engine details and the structure are evident.
(James P Church)

The armour firewall, showing the slightly lighter zinc-chromate inset panel and stencil markings.
*(**Midwest Aero Restorations**)*

*The armour plate from 'Jumpin Jacques' ahead of the glycol coolant header tank fitted above and behind the propeller. (**Steve Atkin**)*

The oil tank and plumbing in front of the armoured firewall on 'Jumpin Jacques'
*(**Steve Atkin**)*

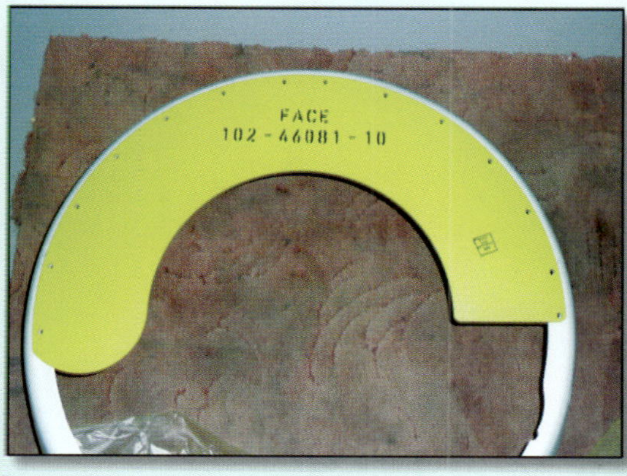

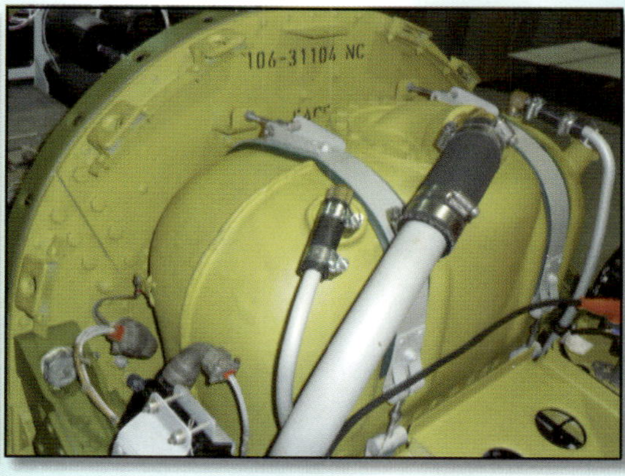

***Opposite page top:** The starboard side of the engine on 'Happy Jack's Go Buggy' during installation. Note the different colours on the mounts, and the blanking plates on the cylinder-head before the exhaust stubs are fitted. These would have been similarly blanked off on newly supplied engines in wartime as well.*

(James P Church)

***Opposite page bottom:** Complete V-1650-7 engine in situ.*

(Mike Jerram via Roger Wallsgrove)

P-51D coolant system flow. Drawings from Pilot's Manual.

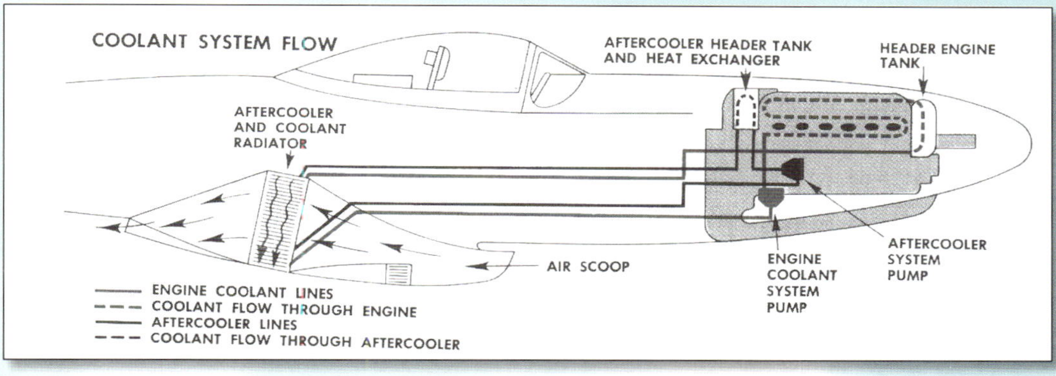

Drawing from Pilot's Manual showing the cooling system.

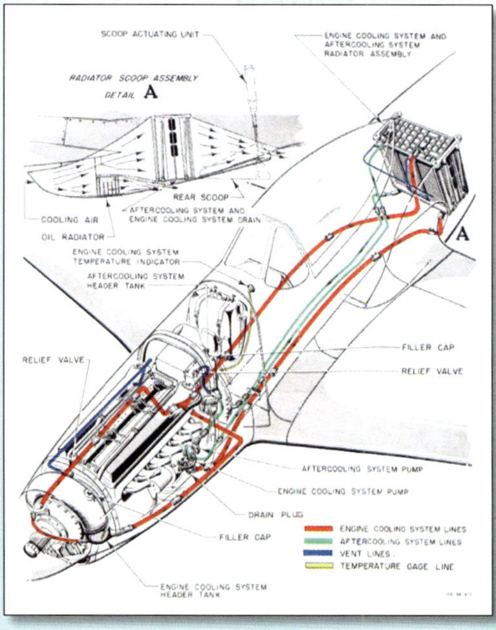

Engine cowling and supports. Drawing from Technical Manual.

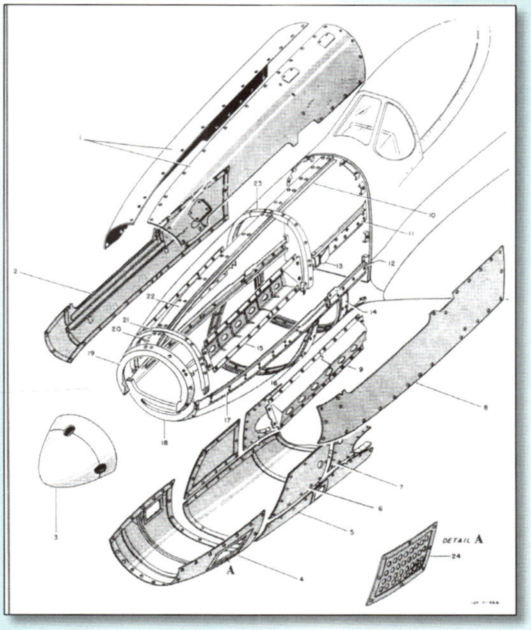

A view of the glycol filler cap inside the flap, with the correct stencils showing on 'Jumpin Jacques'.
(Steve Atkin)

Above, right: *Looking from the port side, this shows the engine to the left, the oil tank (right) and the carburettor and engine control connections on 'Happy Jack's Go Buggy'. Every detail has been replicated to be as faithful to production standard as possible.*
(Midwest Aero Restorations)

Right: *Even the hoses and cables on 'Happy Jack's Go Buggy' replicate war-time colours, stamp and markings.*
(Midwest Aero Restorations)

The oil filler cap and breather inside the flap and with the recreated correct placard showing, on 'Jumpin Jacques'.
(Steve Atkin)

The partly uncowled engine of 'Happy Jack's Go Buggy' reveals a lot of detail, including the carburettor intake trunking.

(Steve Atkin)

Looking from the port side of the aft of the engine bay from above, the silver box is the generator control unit (often removed on modern flying Mustangs), and the hydraulic oil tank beyond with the correct filler cap details.

(Midwest Aero Restorations)

Oil system as shown in Pilot's Manual.

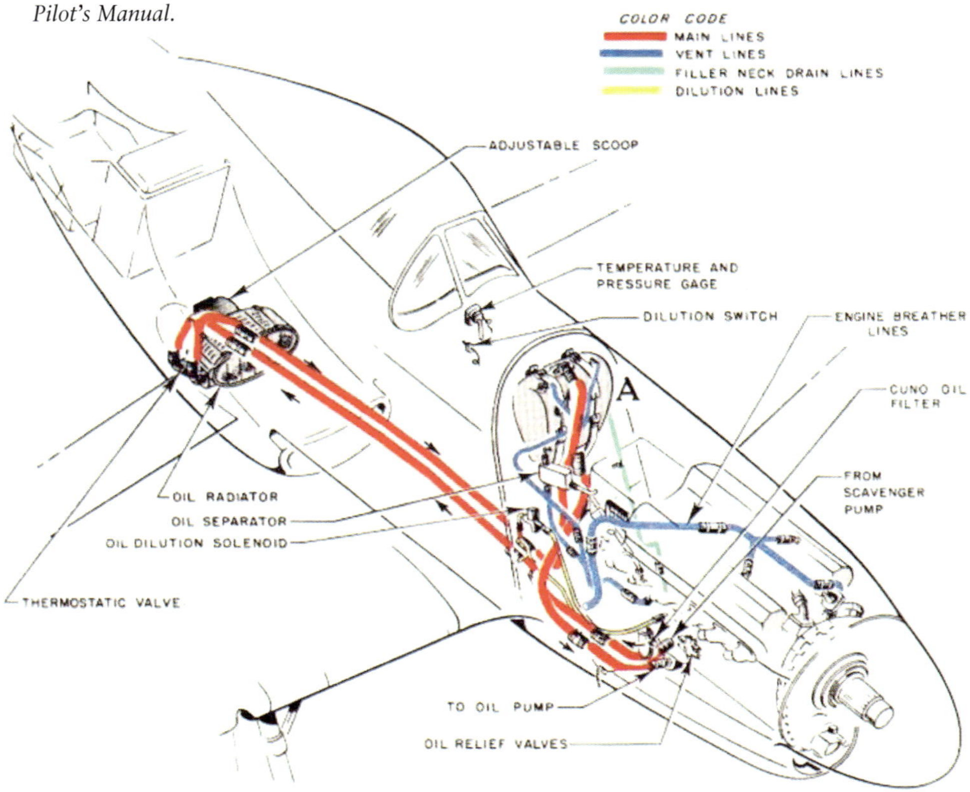

P-51D engine check before test flight. ***(Mike Jerram via Roger Wallsgrove)***

Opposite top: *Details of P-51D engine from the Pilot's Manual.*

Opposite lower: *The exterior of the filtered carburettor intake on CAC Mustang VH-JUC, and the interior, showing the Dzus fasteners for the cowling. Some Mustangs had a blanking plate and no filtered (non-ram) air option.*

(Both James Kightly)

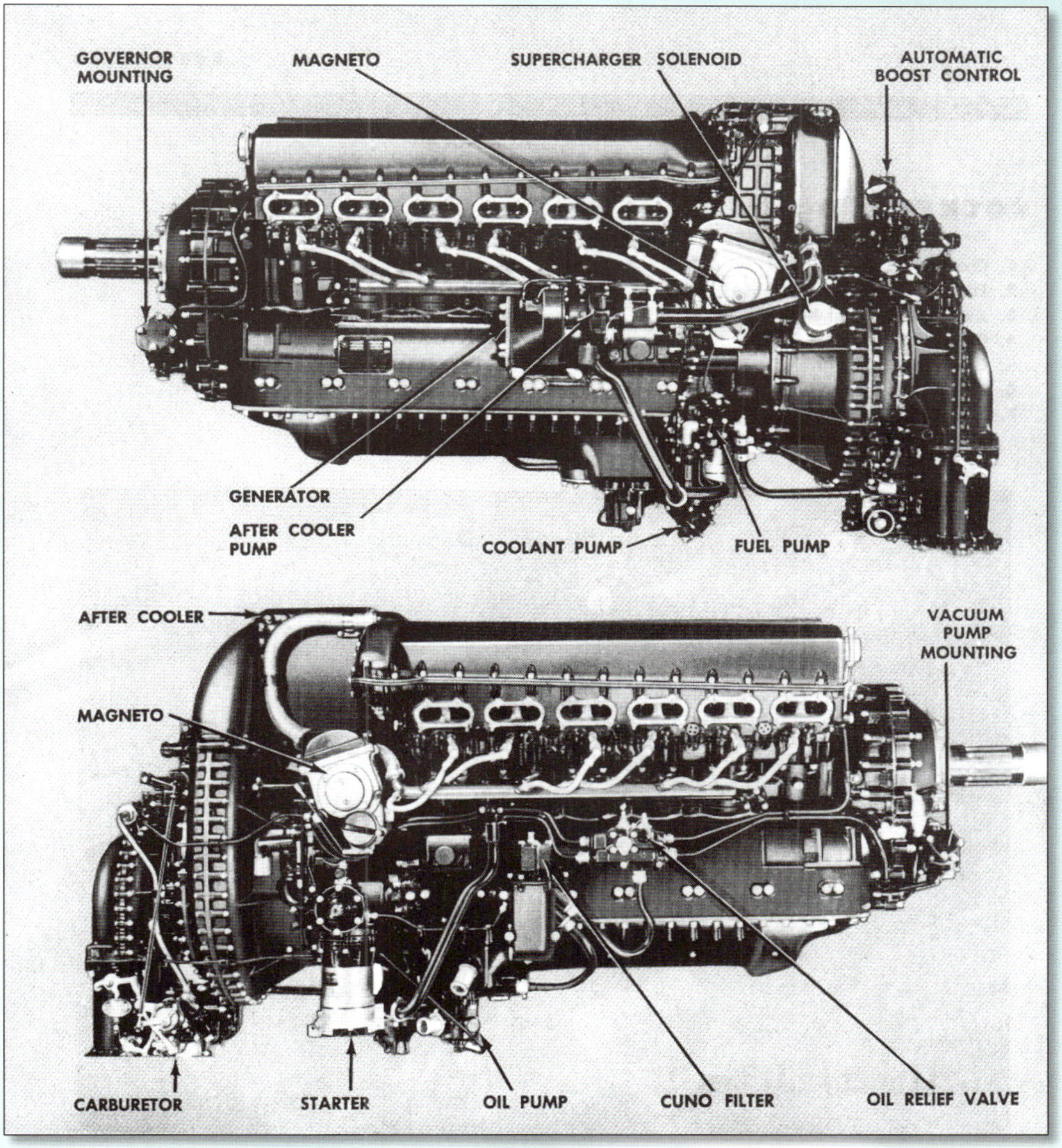
GOVERNOR MOUNTING
MAGNETO
SUPERCHARGER SOLENOID
AUTOMATIC BOOST CONTROL
GENERATOR
AFTER COOLER PUMP
COOLANT PUMP
FUEL PUMP
AFTER COOLER
VACUUM PUMP MOUNTING
MAGNETO
CARBURETOR
STARTER
OIL PUMP
CUNO FILTER
OIL RELIEF VALVE

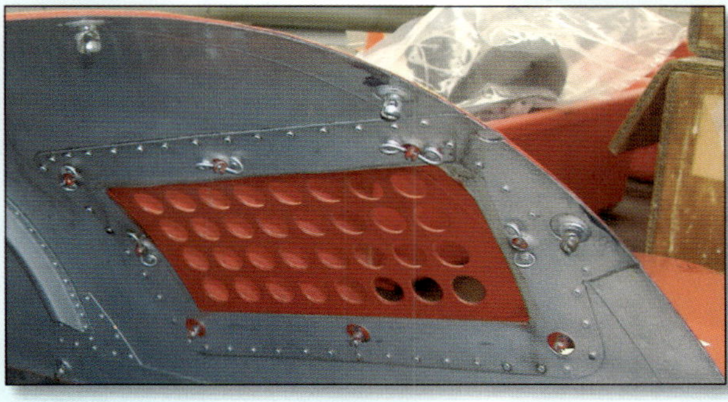

***This Page:** Three views of the engine cowlings. Note the chequers in the lower photograph wrap inside the carburettor air intake.*
*(**All Stratus**)*

***Opposite:** Two views of the area aft of the engine, on the RAAF Museum's CAC Mustang (top) and 'Happy Jack's Go Buggy' below.*
*(**James Kightly & Steve Atkin**)*

*Further photos of the engine cowling. Note the varied sheen of the natural metal. (**All Stratus**)*

The markings and stencils on the cuffed propeller on 'Happy Jack's Go Buggy'. Note the access panel on the boss.
(James P Church)

Middle, left: The spinner backplate.
(Steve Atkin)

***Above and left**: The markings and stencils on the un-cuffed propeller on 'Jumpin Jacques'.*
(Steve Atkin)

Two photos of the Hamilton Standard propeller, top with the 'cuffed' blade, lower with the cuff not fitted.

(All Stratus)

Two more views of the Hamilton Standard propeller with cuffs fitted. ***(Stratus & James Kightly)***

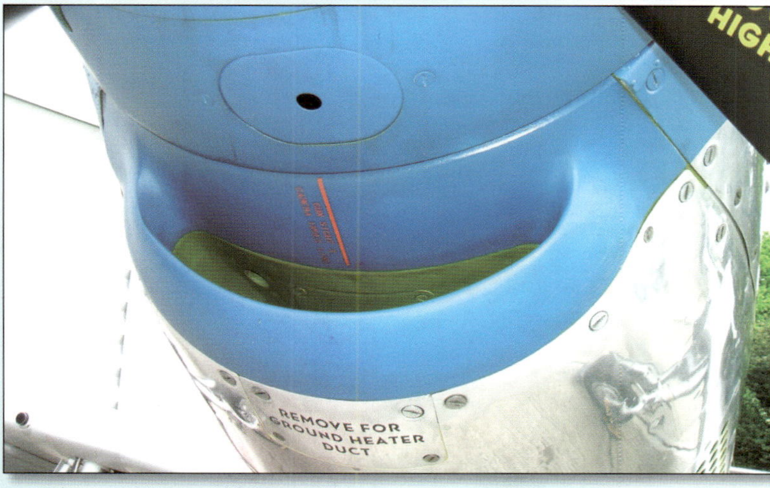

The carburettor intake showing stencil details on P-51D-20NA 'Jumpin Jaques' 44-72035 (G-SIJJ). ***(Steve Atkin)***

Canopy & Cockpit

Above: *Front view of the windscreen.*
Below: *Rear view of the canopy. Internal frame is visible.*

(All Stratus)

P-51D hood in the open position. In cockpit Capt. Raymound H. Littge, a 352nd Fighter Group flight leader. *(USAF)*

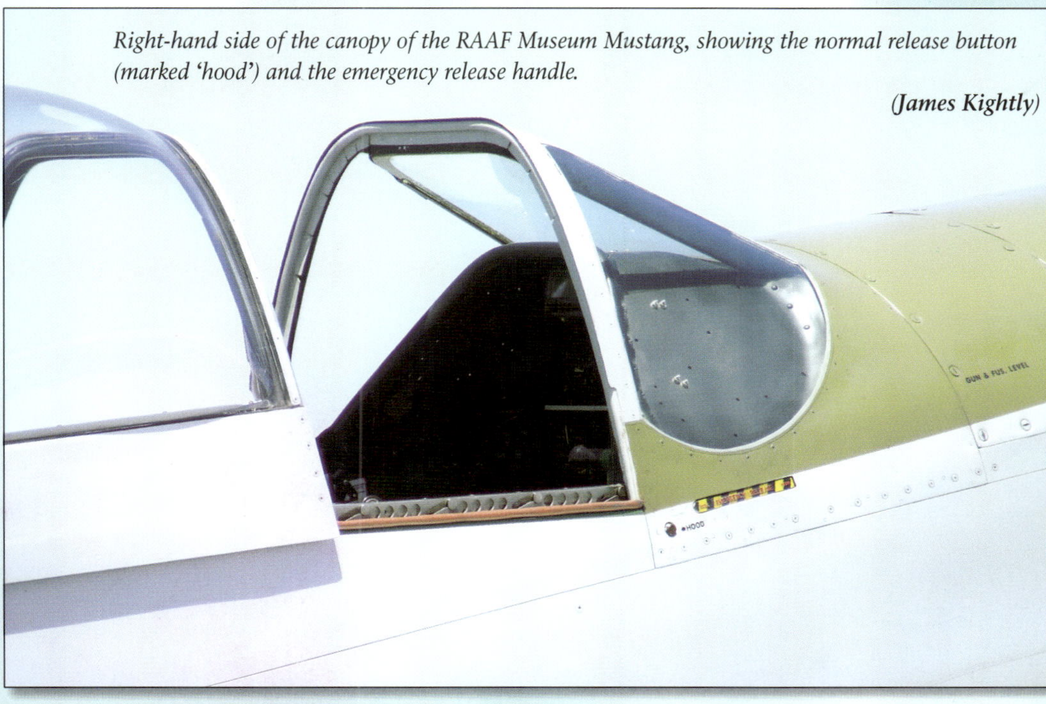

Right-hand side of the canopy of the RAAF Museum Mustang, showing the normal release button (marked 'hood') and the emergency release handle. *(James Kightly)*

Canopy hood frame and pilot's head armour froom the rear.

(Stratus)

Opposite page top: *Drawing from Technical Manual showing canopy details.*

Opposite page bottom: *Canopy frame with canopy glazing removed.*

(James Kightly)

Windsreen front view. K-14A gunsight is also visible.

(Stratus)

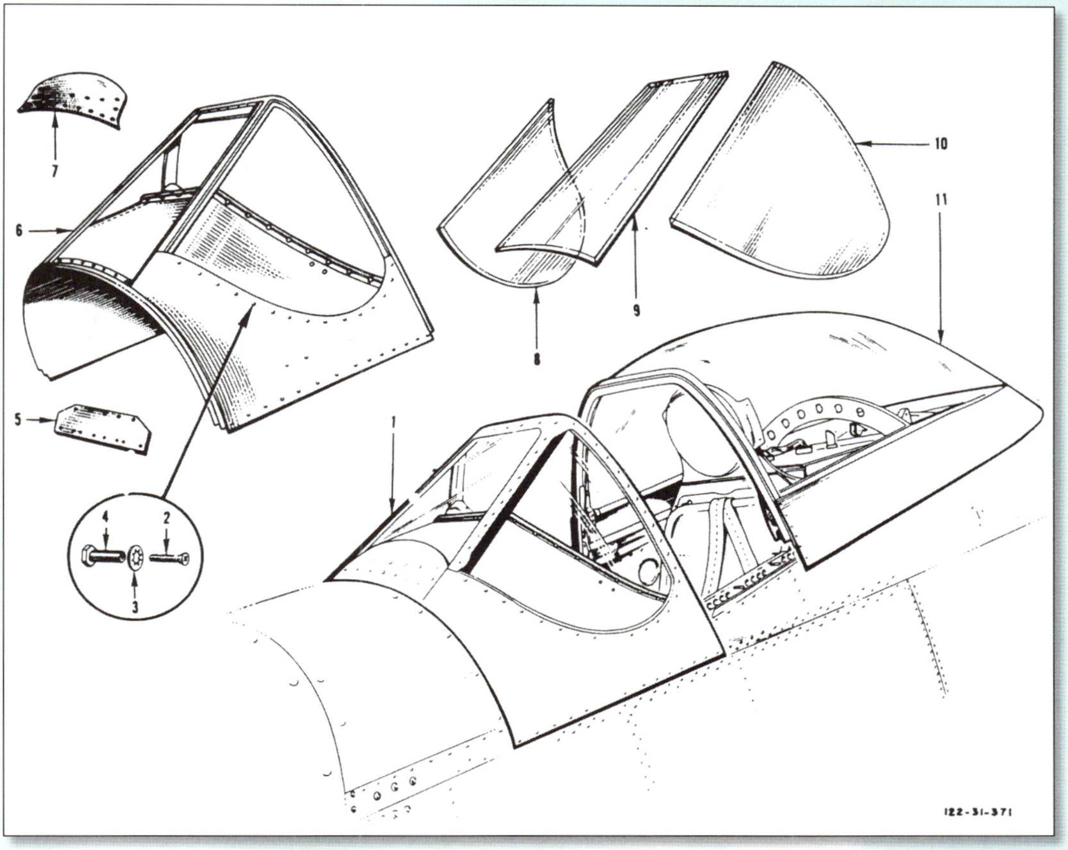
7
6
5
4
2
3
8
9
10
11
1
122-31-371

FLAMMABLE
LIQUIDS
NO SMOKING
KEEP HEAT
AND FIRE AWAY

A good view of the cockpit area of 'Happy Jack's Go Buggy'. The dual rear view mirrors as preferred by Jack Ilfrey are visible on the canopy top.
(James P Church)

A wide-angle overall view of the cockpit in 'Happy Jack's Go Buggy'.
(James P Church)

A view of the main instrument panel of Happy Jacks Go Buggy', with the lower armament panel visible behind the stick.
(James P Church)

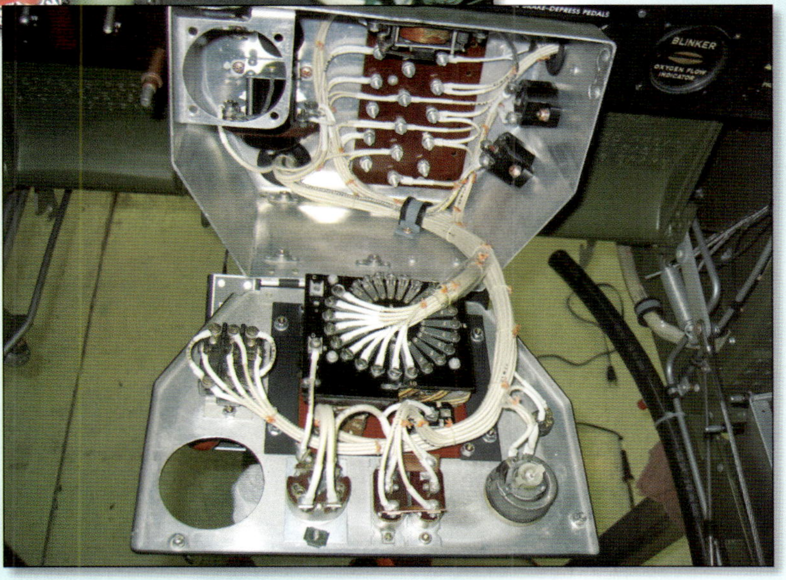

The interior wiring of that panel.
(Midwest Aero Restorations)

The original, working K-14 computing gun sight nicknamed the 'No Miss-um' in service.

(James P Church)

Opposite page: *Two views of the area behind the pilot's seat, with the canopy removed, but with the seat and pilot's back and headrest armour in place. One for the show judges, this area is rarely fitted out correctly, and most preserved Mustangs have none of this equipment. Compare this with the same area in the Smithsonian Museum's Mustang, fitted with the earlier BC-457 Transmitter as seen on page 100.*

(Both Midwest Aero Restorations)

A slightly different armament panel shown on CAC built Mustang VH-JUC.

(James Kightly)

The seat and harness removed from 'Happy Jack's Go Buggy'.

(James P Church)

The interior of the National Museum of the USAF's P-51D cockpit is an original, heavily worn example. Obtained from the West Virginia ANG in 1957, 44-74936 was the last Mustang assigned to a USAF tactical unit. **(NMUSAF)**

Preserved instrument panel of a CAC Mustang in the RAAF Museum. ***(James Kightly)***

Instrument panel. Late versions of P-51D. Photo from Pilot's Manual.

1. *Selector Dimmer Controls*
2. *Remote Indicator Compass*
3. *Clock*
4. *Suction Gauge*
5. *Manifold Pressure Gauge*
6. *Airspeed Indicator*
7. *Directional Gyro*
8. *Artificial Horizon*
9. *Carburetor Air Temperature*
10. *Coolant Temperature*
11. *Tachometer*
12. *Altimeter*
13. *Bank-and-Turn Indicator*
14. *Rate-of-Climb Indicator*
15. *Oil Temperature, Fuel and Oil Pressure Gauge*
16. *Engine Control Panel*
17. *Landing Gear Warning Light*
18. *Parking Brake*
19. *Oxygen Flow Blinker*
20. *Oxygen Pressure Gauge*
21. *Ignition Switch*
22. *Bomb and Rocket Switch*
23. *Chemical Release Switch*
24. *Cockpit Light Control*
25. *Gun, Camera and Sight Switch*
26. *Rocket Control Panel*
27. *Fuel Shut-off Valve*
28. *Fuel Selector Valve*
29. *Emergency Hydraulic Release*

Drawing of K-14 computing gunsight from Pilot's Manual.

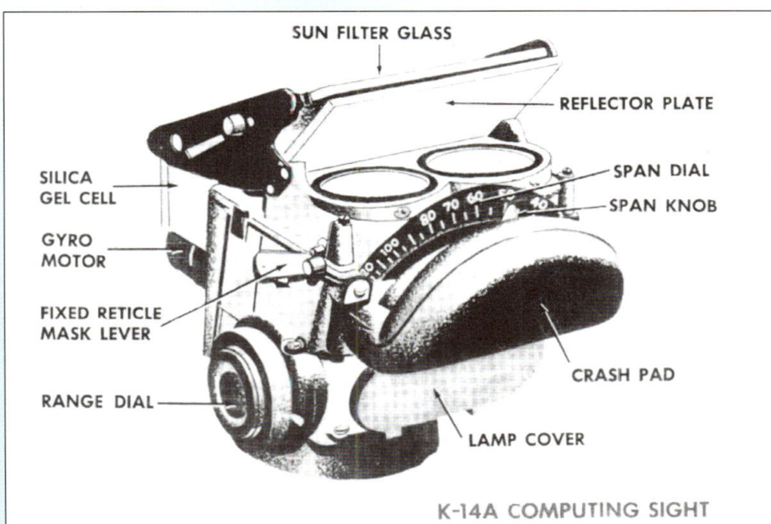

Above: *Capt. Kirke B. Everson is sitting in the cockpit of his P-51D, serial 44-14372, 5Q-E 'Mary Beth', of the 504th FS, 339th FG, April 1945. Note the unusual (P-38 style) mirror in the canopy. (USAF)*

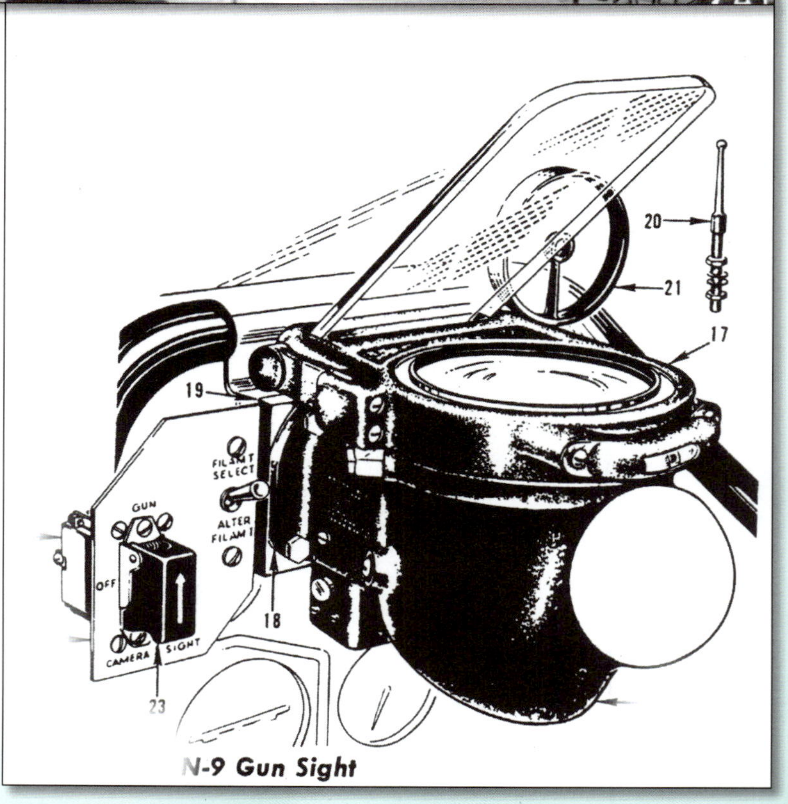

Drawing of the N-9 Gunsight used on the early P-51D. Drawing from Technical Manual.

Two wartime photos of the early P-51D cockpit.
(*Mike Jerram via Roger Wallsgrove*)

Pilot's seat and the lower part of the control column. **(Stratus)**

Port side console and throttle quadrant. **(Stratus)**

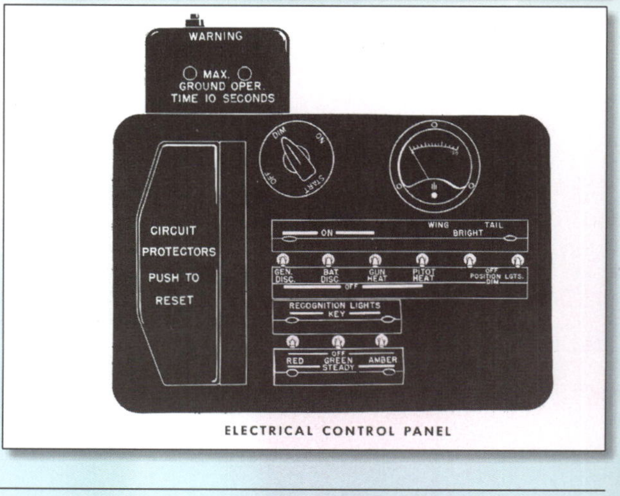

ELECTRICAL CONTROL PANEL

Drawing of Electrical Control Panel as shown in Pilot's Manual.

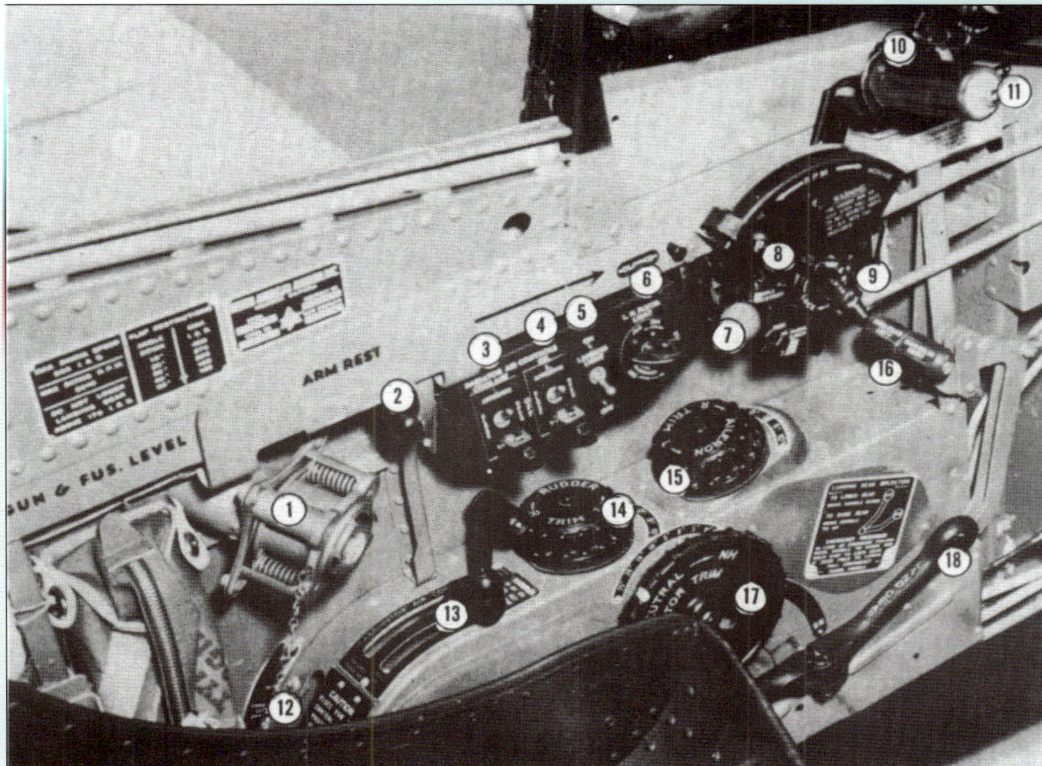

Above: *Port console. Late versions of P-51D. Photo from Pilot's Manual.*

Below: *Throttle Quadrant as shown in the Pilot's Manual.*

1. Flare Pistol Opening
2. Cockpit Light
3. Coolant Radiator Air Control Switch
4. Oil Radiator Air Control Switch
5. Landing Light Switch
6. Left Fluorescent Light Switch
7. Mixture Control
8. Propeller Control
9. Throttle Quadrant Locks
10. Throttle
11. Microphone Button
12. Flap Control Handle
13. Carburetor Air Controls
14. Rudder Trim Tab Control
15. Aileron Trim Tab Control
16. Bomb Salvo Releases
17. Elevator Trim Tab Control
18. Landing Gear Control

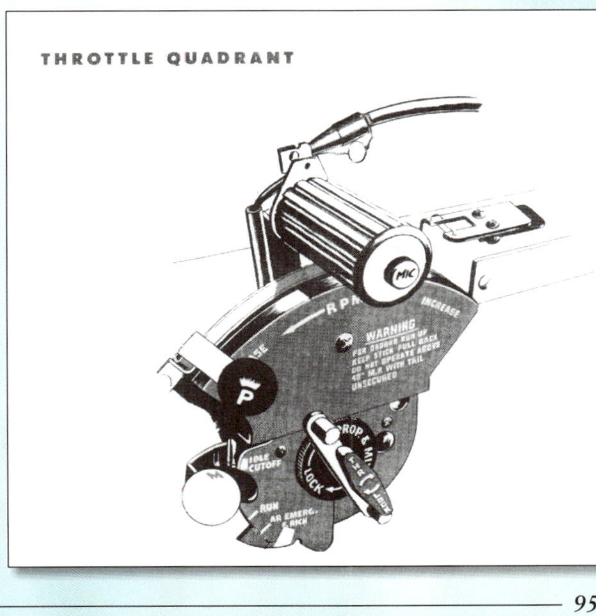

Details of the Throttle quadrant assembly. Drawings from Technical Manual.

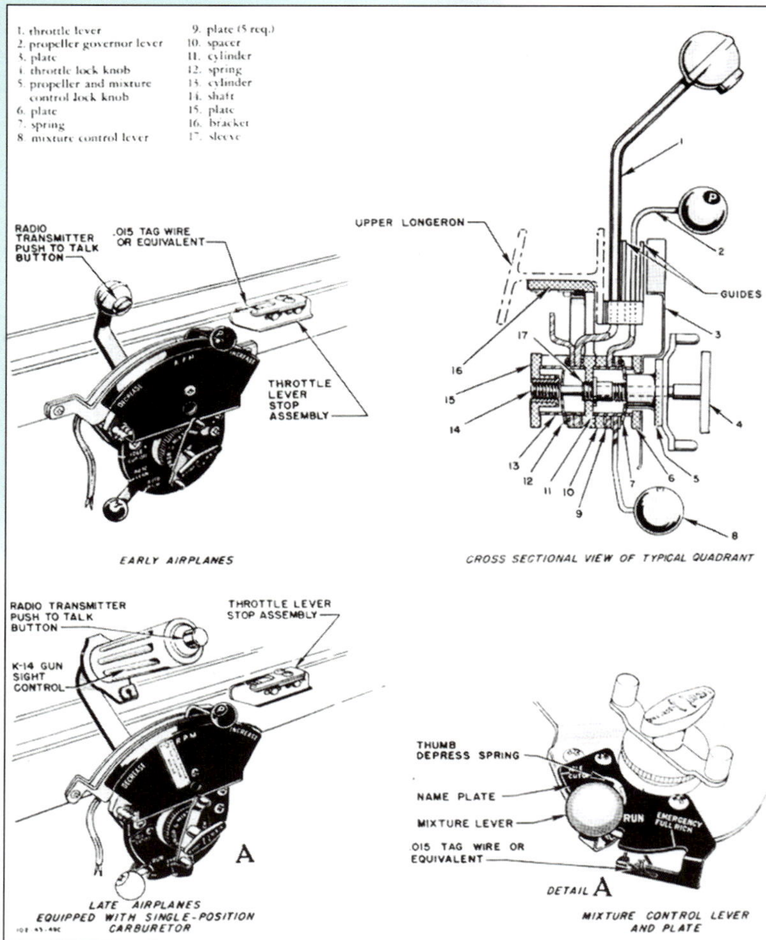

Bottom, left: Bomb release.

Bottom, right: Fuel tank gauge.

Drawings from Pilot's Manual

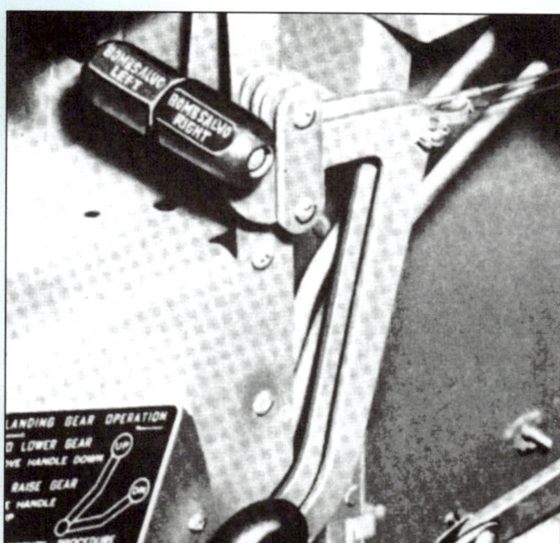

Right panel. Late versions of P-51D. Photo from Pilot's Manual.

1. Oxygen Regulator
2. Emergency Canopy Release
3. Recognition Light Key
4. Canopy Crank and Lock
5. Circuit Breakers (under)
6. Right Fluorescent Light Switch
7. Electrical Control Panel
8. Rear Warning Radar Control Panel
9. VHF Volume Control Knob
10. VHF Control Box
11. IFF Control Panel
12. Detonator Buttons
13. Detrola Control Box
14. Cockpit Light

Rocket Control Panel. Photo from Pilot's Manual.

ENGINE LIMITATIONS
TAKE OFF CONDITIONS
U.S. ARMY
AIR FORCES
OXYGEN DURATION
AN/APS-13
EMERGENCY

WARNING
COOLANT
RPM
CLIMB
PARK BRAKE
PARKING BRAKE INSTRUCTIONS
BLINKER
OIL PRESSURE
DELAY
EMERGENCY

Opposite page top: *The various placards (here on 'Happy Jack's Go Buggy') as originally fitted on the starboard side are evident, and the control box for the (working) AN/APS-13 tail warning radar can be seen just below the canopy handle. Note that the seat is removed in this picture. (**Midwest Aero Restorations**)*

Opposite page bottom: *The main panel, fully fitted out. Among numerous other details, the NAA rudder pedal casting can be seen.*

*(**Midwest Aero Restorations**)*

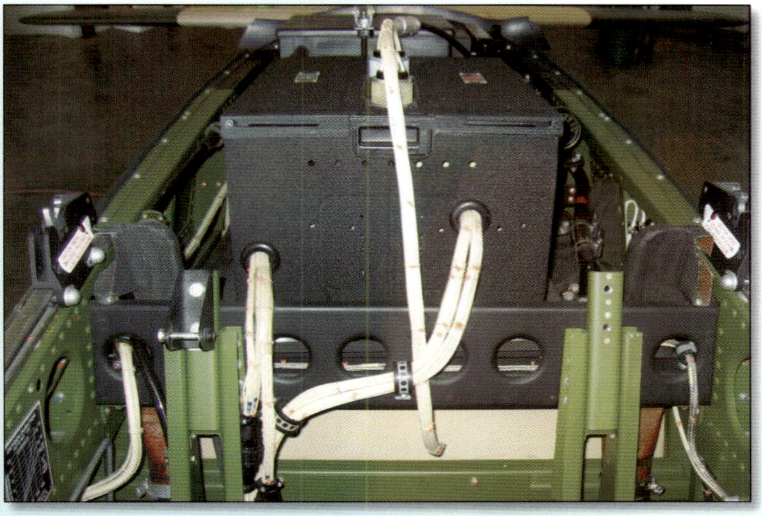

Top: *The trim controls, landing and flap gear. Again, every effort has been taken to ensure this is as complete and accurate as possible.*
*(**Midwest Aero Restorations**)*

Left: *The Bendix Radio (and battery) behind the pilot's seat. Again, note how tidy, yet varied the cockpit interior is. The seat (and armour) are removed in this picture.*
*(**Midwest Aero Restorations**)*

P-51D rear part of the cockpit from above. Note this example (at the Smithsonian) does not have the cross brace beam seen previously, but does have the aerial leading through the canopy. ***(Stratus)***

Radio Installation (electrical connections) in Early P-51D Versions.

1. *Throttle Switch*
2. *BC-442 Antenna Relay*
3. *106-71154 Panel Assembly*
4. *SCR-515-A Detonator Buttons*
5. *BC-451-A Transmitter Control Box*
6. *BC-450-A Receiver Control Box*
7. *FL-B Filter Box*
8. *SCR-516-A Control Box*
9. *BC-457 Transmitter*
10. *BC-453 Receiver*
11. *Battery*
12. *MC-385 Microphone Adaptor*
13. *BC-456 Modulator Unit*
14. *Indicator Lights SCR-515*
15. *Inertia Switch SCR-515*
16. *SCR-515-A Radio Set*
17. *BC-456 Transmitter*
18. *BC-455 Receiver*
19. *BC-454 Receiver*
20. *106-71131 Channel Support*
21. *109-71132 Channel Support*
22. *SCR-274-N Antenna*

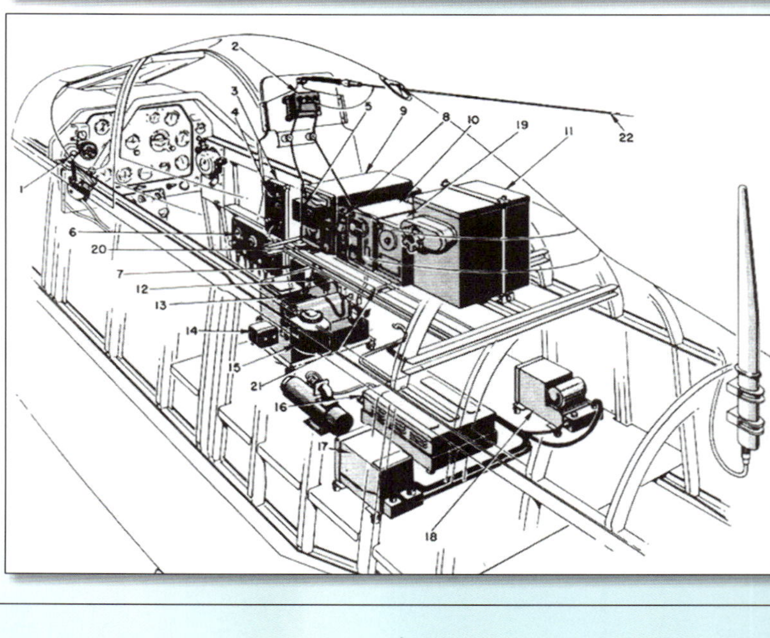

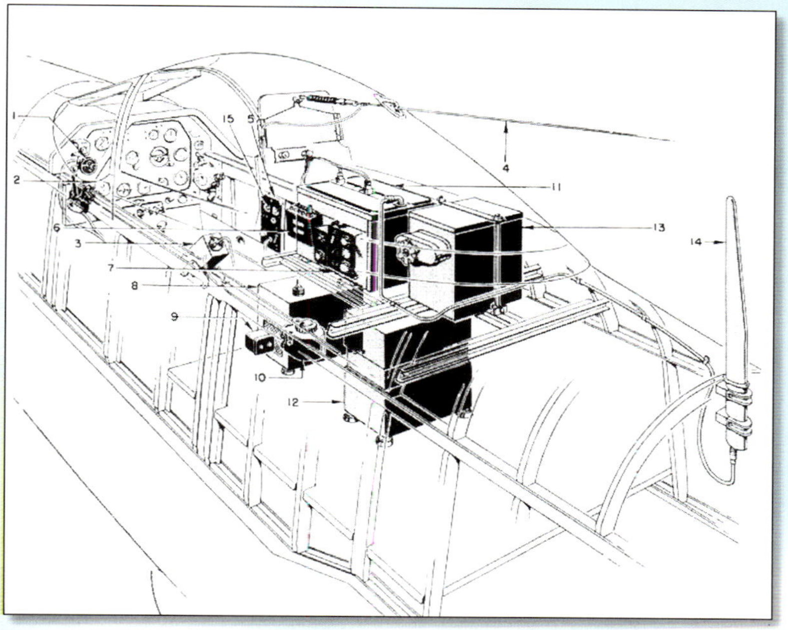

Radio Installation in late P-51D versions.

1. Remote Contactor
2. Throttle Switch
3. Detrola Receiver Model-4J8
4. Detrola & SCR-274-N Antenna
5. I06-71154 Panel Assembly
6. Control Box For SCR-522-A
7. Control Box For SCR-595-A
8. Dynamotor For SCR-522-A
9. Indicator Lamps SCR-695
10. Inertia Switch SCR-695
11. Transmitter Receiver SCR-522-A
12. Radio Set SCR-695-A
13. Battery
14. Antenna For SCR-522-A
15. SCR-695-A Detonator Buttons

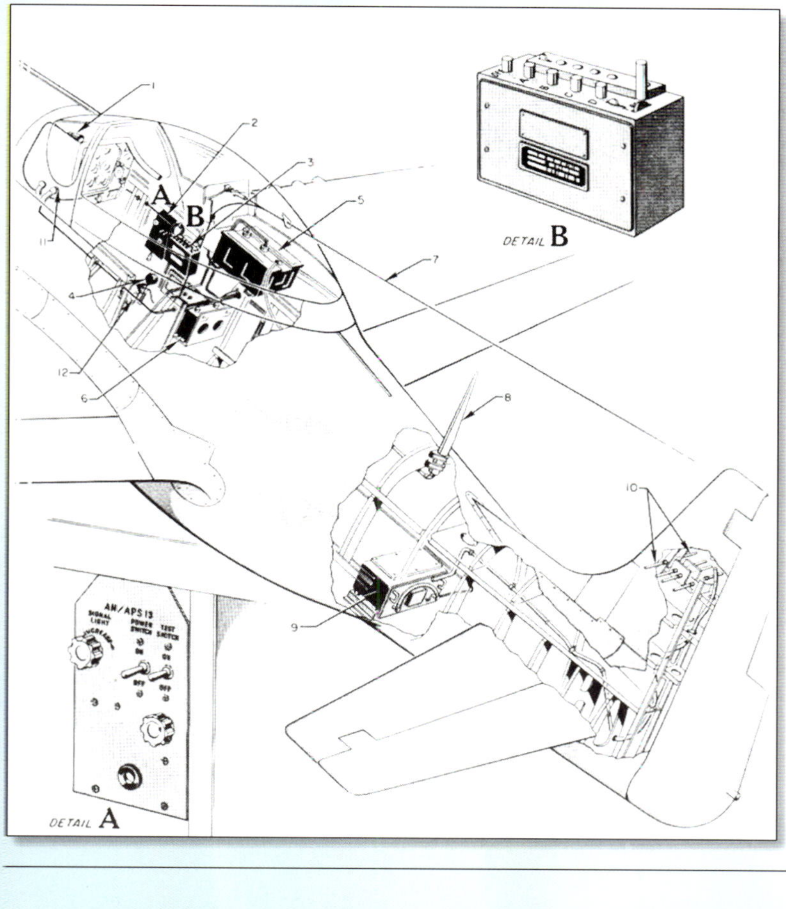

Radio Installation with AN-APS-13 system in late P-51D versions.

1. AN/APS-13 Radio signal lights
2. AN/APS-13 Control Panel
3. SCR-522-A Radio Control Panel
4. AN/APS-13 Radio Signal Bell
5. SCR-522-A Radio Set
6. Dynamotor for SCR-522-A
7. Antenna
8. Mast for SCR-522-A
9. AN/APS-13 Radio Set
10. Antenna Array for AN/APS-13
11. Throttle Switch
12. Radio Range Receiver

Tail

Top: *The stabiliser set.* **(Stratus)** **Below:** *The Vintage Wings of Canada Mustang's tail when jacked and trestled for engine removal. Note the weights and jack position.* ***(James Kightly)***

Starboard horizontal stabiliser from above. Note the Antenna Array for AN/APS-13.

Port horizontal stabiliser with metal covered elevator. Note elevator trim tab.

Another photo of starboard side of the horizontal stabiliser.

(All Stratus)

Close up view of the elevator and mass balance.
(Stratus)

The An/APS-13 tail-warning radar aerials in the fin. They are parallel, despite the impression given by the wide angle lens.
(James Kightly)

The vertical stabiliser of CAC Mustang VH-JUC, showing configuration, camouflage (3 Squadron RAAF 'Southern Cross') and ventral aerial.
(James Kightly)

Above: *the rudder trim-tab actuator.*
(Stratus)

The highly finished stabilisers on 'Daddy's Girl' a previous restoration by Midwest Aero. Rarely, if ever, would combat Mustangs be polished to this degree, although they were both kept clean and reasonably well buffed by the crew.
(James P Church)

Photo of the stabiliser-fin fillet, starboard side.
(Stratus)

LANDING GEAR

Above: *P-51D-20-NA landing gear and wheel well details. Landing lamp and hudraulic pipes are also visible.*

(Mike Jerram via Roger Wallsgrove)

Left: *Inner side of the main wheel.*

(Stratus)

Above:** A general view of the main gear on VH-JUC. **(James Kightly)
***Below:** This photograph during the restoration of 'Happy Jack's Go Buggy' shows the gear bay interior clearly, but also the uncovered wing joint and the unpainted wing centre section underside with the 'watermarks' on the metal visible. The NAA finishing manual instructed staff not to bother to remove such marks.*
(Midwest Aero Restorations)

Details of the main wheel well and surrounding area on 'Happy Jack's Go Buggy', and (Below) the 'Menasco' oleo marking. Menasco Manufacturing Company also supplied landing gear oleos to North American Aviation and the parts were interchangeable with the original Bendix 'Pneudraulic' type.

(Steve Atkin)

Right: *Accurately represented markings and finish on main gear shock strut. The marks on the chromed section vanish once the strut is in use.*

(James P Church)

*The landing light on VH-JUC (**James Kightly**) and 'Happy Jack's Go Buggy'.*
(Midwest Aero Restorations)

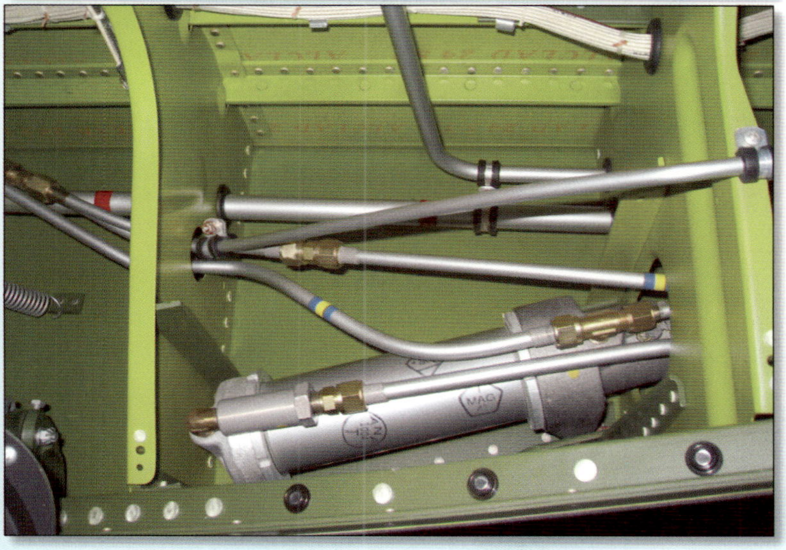

The port gear hydraulic ram. All the details, stamps, blue-yellow or red pipe markings and cabling is as accurate as can be made. The edge of the landing light can be seen bottom left.
(Midwest Aero Restorations)

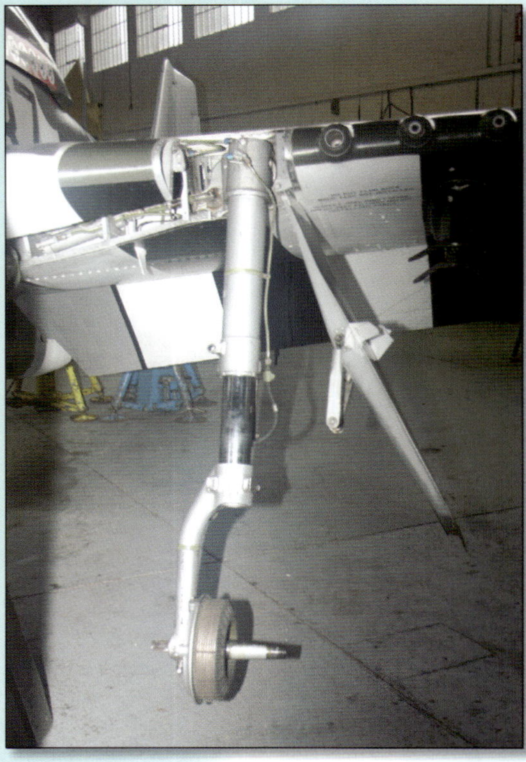

Three views of the main gear leg. Note the attachment-point in the top left photo.

***Bottom left**: Close up view of the main leg attachment to the wing spar.*

(All Stratus)

Above left: *Outside view of the starboard main landing gear.*

Above right: *Inner view of the starboard main landing gear. Details of the door mounting are visible.*

Bottom left: *Outside view of the main landing gear wheel.*

(All Stratus)

The inner end of the port wheel well of 'Happy Jack's Go Buggy' showing the extensive 'spaghetti' in this area, and slight variations in zinc chromate green on different parts. Zinc chromate was not a colour, but a treatment, so the hue varied depending on the material, mix, use and batch. ***(Midwest Aero Restorations)***

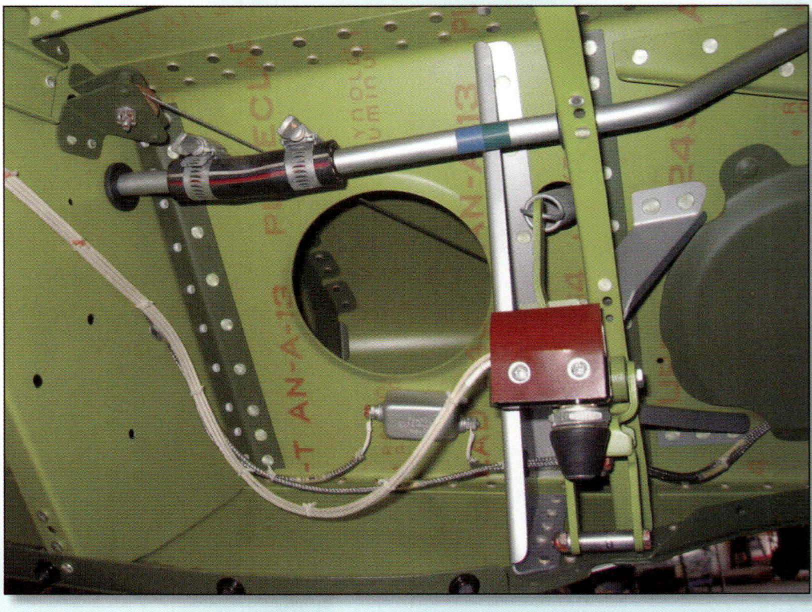

Looking forward from inside the port wheel well on the same aircraft with the red watermarking on the alloy sheet showing through the zinc chromate. ***(Midwest Aero Restorations)***

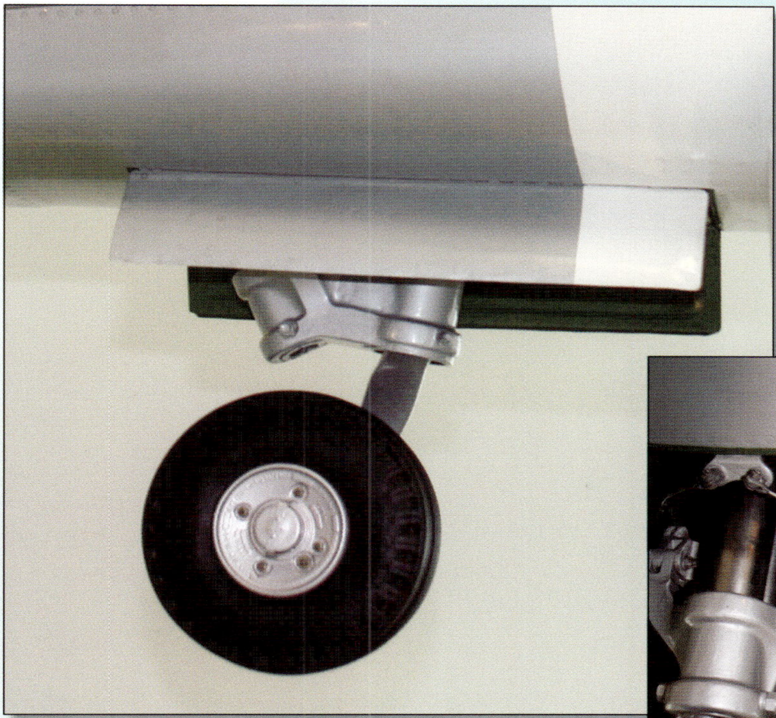

Top: *Starboard side of the tail wheel.*

Above: *Tail wheel oleo strut. The green is not original.*

Left: *Port side of the tail wheel.*

(All Stratus)

Photo of the tail wheel showing the 'at rest' position.
(James Kightly)

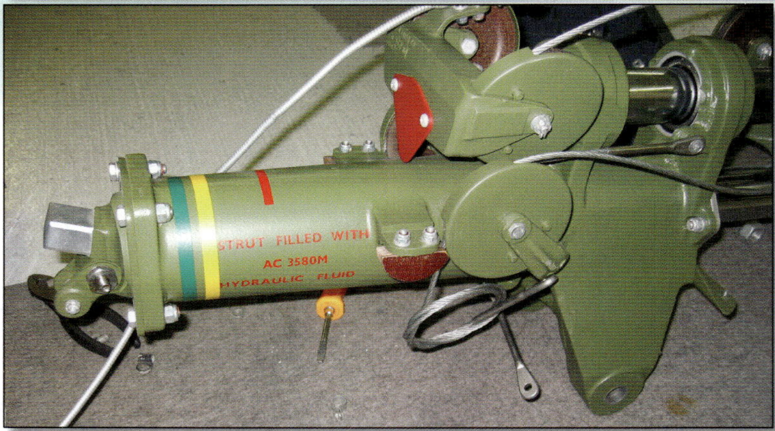

The tail gear actuating strut. The wheel is off to the right, and when fitted the mounting at the bottom of the photo is to the rear.
(Midwest Aero Restorations)

The interior of the tail section showing the gear door, piano-hinge, inspector's stamps and fabric patches over the lightening/inspection holes. Note also the plain watermarked alloy sheeting above.
(Midwest Aero Restorations)

Armament Ordinance & Drop Tanks

Armourers of 364th FG working on P-51D wing, England 1945. *(USAF)*

Photo from Technical Manual showing the gun installation.

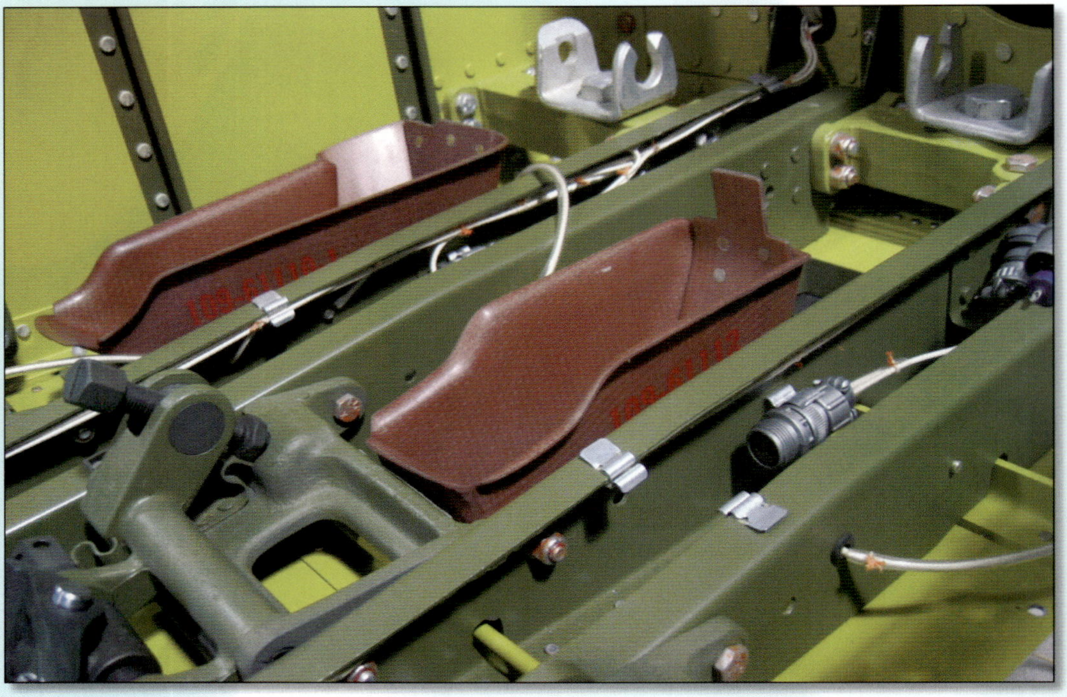

Above: *The interior of the gun bay, without the guns. The ejection chute guides (made of moulded phenolic resin sheet) and gun mountings as well as the electrical triggers are seen as a result.*

(Midwest Aero Restorations)

Middle: *The port wing gun barrels on the Canadian Aviation Museum Mustang.*

(James Kightly)

The gun muzzles and rack on 'Happy Jack's Go Buggy' Note the soft demarcation to the Olive Drab green applied (as originally on this aircraft) over the invasion stripes. The sway braces are fitted to the rack here.

(James P Church)

Above: *Gun bay details without guns fitted (**James Kightly**) and (**Below**) with guns, ammunition, chutes, firing solenoids etc all fitted. (**Steve Atkin**)*

Above: *Gunsight indexing marking on the cowling underside, aft of the spinner.*

*(**Steve Atkin**)*

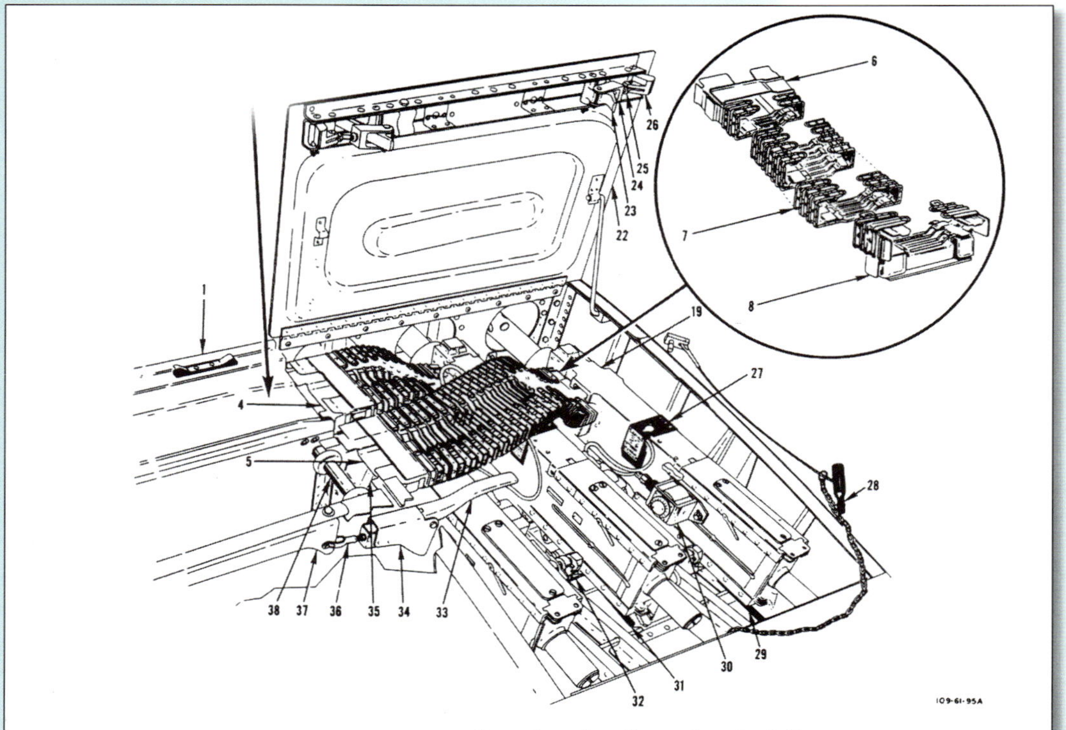

Figure 94—Wing Guns Installation (Part 1 of 2)

***Left**: Armourer with a Mustang machine gun. Note the spring-loaded barrel mounting. Photo taken in Italy 1945*
(USAF)

Below: 500lb bomb fitted to the P-51D bomb rack. Note how rough (and dirty) the bomb's finish is.
(USAF)

***Opposite page top**: Drawing of the machine gun instalation. Technical Manual.*
***Opposite page bottom**: Armourers of the 504th Armament Group at work putting ammunition belts in a P-51D in England, September 1944.*
(USAF)

Armourers of 503rd Armament Group at work, loading bombs on P-51D, England, September 1944. Note the drop tank under the port wing.
(USAF)

Photos of rockets and mountings on the Australian War Memorial Mustang (right) and airworthy Mustang VH-BOB. These are the HVAR rocket with a 5" rocket engine fitted. This was to regain the velocity lost with the adoption of a five inch shell to a 3.5" engine; in the end it turned out even faster than the regular 3.5" rocket, which resulted in its designation as High-Velocity Aircraft Rocket, or HVAR. These were used by the RAAF in Korea.
(James Kightly)

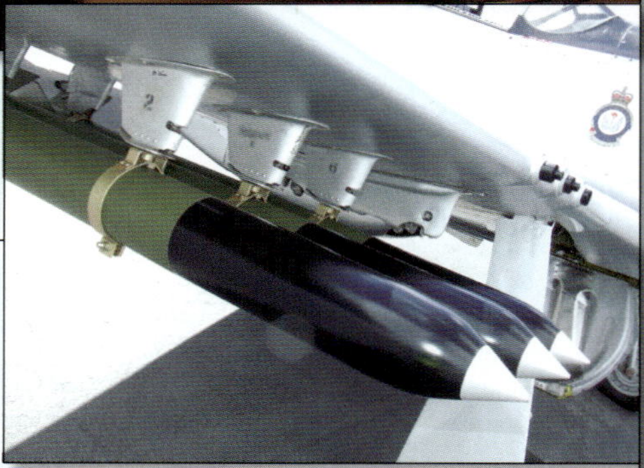

Two photos showing the P-51D bomb rack.
(All Stratus)

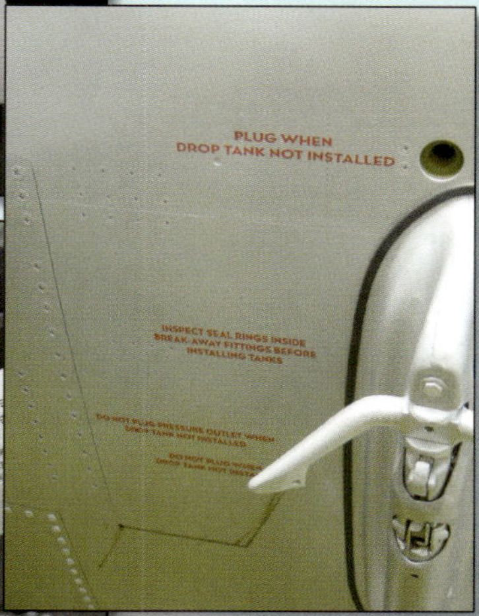

Above: *The wing stencil markings by the wing rack recreated on 'Daddy's Girl'.*

Left: *Bomb rack under the starboard wing with a replica impregnated paper drop tank, as seen on 'Happy Jack's Go Buggy'. Details overleaf.*
(Steve Atkin)

One of the 108 US gallon treated-paper drop tank replicas used on 'Happy Jack's Go Buggy'. These tanks are fully plumbed and operational, and were manufactured from a mould of an original owned by Bob Baker, by Roush Aviation. Mike VadeBonCoeur explains: "There was a mold made right off the original, so our tanks have every imperfection that the originals would have had, the size, except these are made out of a fiberglass, carbon fiber and Kevlar combination for support, and are thus much stronger and durable. It is our understanding that you had about six hours that you could have fuel in the tanks before they would start to deteriorate. So they would put fuel in them and immediately go fly the mission, dropping them never to be seen again."
(James P Church)

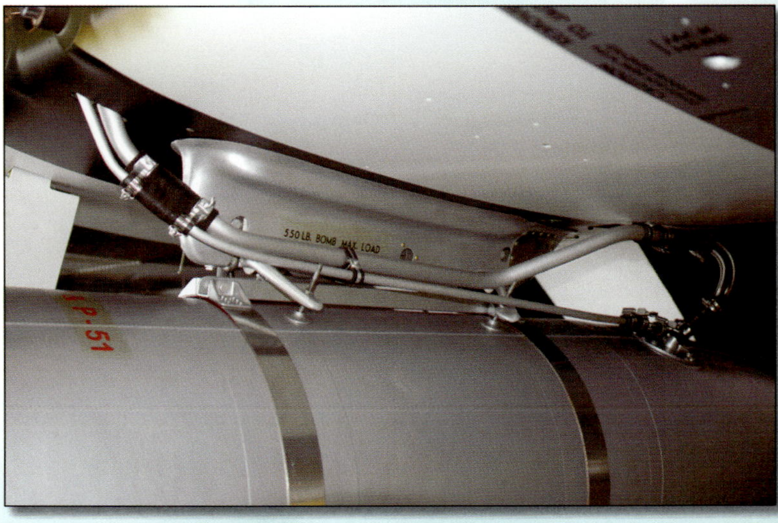

Here is a close-up of the plumbing detail for the paper tanks. Notice the glass segments meant to break away when the tanks are released.
(James P Church)

Top: *P-51D-15-NA, serial 44-14495, 'Dallas Doll' of 352nd FS, personal aircraft of Lt. Frank H Bouldin Jr. Note the stained white on the star and bar and front D-Day stripe from dirt adhering to the fuel spills on the fuselage.* ***(USAF)***

Middle: *Another view of the recreated paper tank on 'Happy Jack's Go Buggy' (Steve Atkin)*

Bottom: *'Lefty' Groves' P-51D undergoing an engine test at Debden. Note the 108 US Gallon paper tanks, oil streak on the cowling and covered gunports.* ***(F M Grove)***

Fitting of the 75 gal drop tank. Photo taken in England 1944.

(USAF)

Lt. William P. Hess of the 384th FS, 364th FG, poses beside his P-51D-15-NA, serial 44-15202, 5Y•H 'Bergie III' at an 8th AF base, probably Honington England, 15 December 1944.

(USAF)

P-51D-20-NA, serial 44-72218, WZ•I, "Big Beautiful Doll" of 84th FS, 8th AF, personal aircraft of Col. John D. Landers.

P-51D-20-NA, serial 44-63777, "209", "Three of a Kind" of 21st FG 46th FS, Iwo Jima.

P-51D-20-NA, serial 44-7205, "66", "The Flying Undertaker", "Snooks" of 82nd TRS, 71 TRG, Binmaley, February 1945. Personal aircraft of Maj. William Shomo.

F-51D-30-NA , *serial 44-75728 of 67th FBS, 18th FBW, USAAF, Pilot - Maj. Arnold 'Moon' Mullins. On 5th February 1951 he shot down DPRKAF Yak-9 over Korea.*

P-51D-5-NA, *serial 44-13298, QP•Q, nicknamed "Marie" of 52nd FG 2nd FS, assigned pilot Freddie Ohr. Aircraft lost on 8th December 1944, with Lt. Paul C. Keyser missing in action over Austria.*

P-51D-5-NA, serial 44-13837, CY•M, 'Miss Marilyn II' of 343rd FS, 55th FG, 8th AF. Pilot - Maj. E. Giller, UK, 1944.

P-51D-10-NA, serial 44-14292, QP•A, "Old Witch" of 334th FS, 4th FG, 8th AF. Pilot - 1st Lt. Robert S. Voyles. Aircraft passed from Lt. Col. Claibourne H. Kinnard Jr. to Lt. Voyles in January 1945.

F-51D-30-NA, serial 44-74522, FF-522 of 131st FBW, Reykjavik, Iceland, September 1952. Overall natural metal with Arctic Red (FS 11105), high visibility markings.

AUSTRALIA

Mustang A68-750 was an American built P-51D supplied to the RAAF (previously 44-84489) and the only RAAF post-war Mustang with shark's teeth, as flown from Iwakuni, Japan, by Squadron Leader R Susans. Today this aircraft is represented by the RAAF Museum's Australian-built CAC Mustang A68-170, which flies in these colours.

Mustang A68-809 was a P-51D delivered to the RAAF in September 1945. It was destroyed when Wing Commander LT 'Lou' Spence of 77 Squadron RAAF was shot down by AA fire over Angang-Ni on operations in Korea in September 1950. It is shown with the RAAF roundel with the post-war reinstated red dot, and with the Wing Commander's pennant below the cockpit. Note the odd serial position and rockets fitted.

A68-141 is a Commonwealth Aircraft Corporation built CA18 Mk.23 Mustang delivered in 1949, and issued to 22 (City of Sydney Citizens Air Force) RAAF Squadron, in 1952, and later to 24 (City of Adelaide) Squadron (shown) in 1956 before being scrapped in 1959. It is one of the few Mustangs seen with the 'Roo' roundel brought in at the end of the aircraft's career with the RAAF.

A formation of 84 Squadron RAAF Mustangs out of Townsville, Queensland in 1945. Squadron Leader Cox's A68-565, LB-V, is a P51-10-NT. The band on the spinner is Insignia Blue.

(RAAF Museum archive.)

BOLIVIA

Mustangs were bought by Bolivia during July of 1954. In 1960, eight former MAP Mustangs from Uruguay were acquired, and six more in 1966. Bolivia also added nine Cavalier F-51Ds (seven F-51Ds and two TF-51Ds) in 1967 and 1968 as part of the US MAP program "PEACE CONDOR".

CANADA

P-51D Mustangs, designated in Canada as 'Tactical Fighter Mark IV', were to equip the following RCAF Auxiliary Fighter Squadrons: 402 'City of Winnipeg' (code AC), 403 'Calgary' (code PR, replaced by AD in 1954), 417 (Central Air Command Composite Flight' (code CB), 420 'City of London' (code AW, replaced by QJ ca. 1955), 424 'City of Hamilton (code BA, replaced by PV in 1954), 442 'City of Vancouver' (code MH) and 443 'Sea Island' (code PF). Mustangs were also used by the Central Flying School [CFS] (code DD), Air Armament School [AAS] (code BZ), No. 1 Flying Training School [FTS] (code GM), Central Experiment & Proving Establishment [CEPE] (code FB) and the Canadian Joint Air Training Center [CJATC] (codes OU and AT).
Profile shows P-51D of 402 Squadron "City of Winnipeg", late '50s.

REPUBLIC OF CHINA:

The Nationalist Chinese Air Force (CNAC) received three squadrons of P-51Ds in 1946. When Chiang Kai-shek's government was overthrown by Mao's Communists in 1949, most of the Nationalist P-51Ds fled to Formosa. However, many were left and were incorporated into the People's Liberation Army Air Force.

CNAC P-51D with tactical code 2101.

P-51D as used by PLAAF (People's Liberation Army Air Force).

COSTA RICA

Four F-51Ds were sold to Costa Rica from the Texas ANG in 1955. The survivors were sold off in March of 1964. Costa Rica never had an air force, and there was no official air force insignia.

CUBA

After Fidel Castro seized control of Cuba in 1959, Cuba's Fuerza Aerea Revolucionaria illegally acquired three ex-civilian Mustangs and they served with the Cuban air force until they were replaced with Russian-built equipment in the early 1960s. FAR F-51D with tactical no 400.

DOMINICAN REPUBLIC

The first P-51s were acquired in 1948, consisting of a mixed batch of six P-51As, P-51Cs, and P-51Ds. In 1952, the Cuerpo de Avacion Militar bought 44 F-51Ds from Sweden. The Dominican Air Force was the last operator of the P-51D when it retired the last 8 samples in 1984, selling them off to private owners Fuerza Aera Dominicana P-51D with tactical no FAD-1923, 1965. Aircraft grey overall.

EL SALVADOR

Seven P-51D Mustangs were brought into service with the Fuerza Aerea Salvadorena (FAS) with obscure origins, mostly bought from private owners. They were added to the six Cavalier Mustangs previously obtained (one TF-51, FAS 400 and five Mustang IIs, FAS 401-405). FAS P-51D of Escuadrilla 1, Escuadron Caza Bombardeo.

FRANCE

The first French unit began its transition to reconnaissance Mustangs in late 1944. In January 1945, the Tactical Reconnaissance Squadron GR II/33 of the French Air Force took their F-6Cs and F-6Ds over Germany on photographic mapping missions. The French Mustangs remained in service until the early 1950s when they were replaced by jet fighters.

P-51D-20-NA 'Annecy', Z (serial 44-72077) ofGR II/33 'Savoie', Armee de l'Air, Cognac, 1952.

GERMANY

The Luftwaffe operated a number of captured P-51D Mustangs for training. P-51D-5 of 2.Staffel of the Versuchsverband.

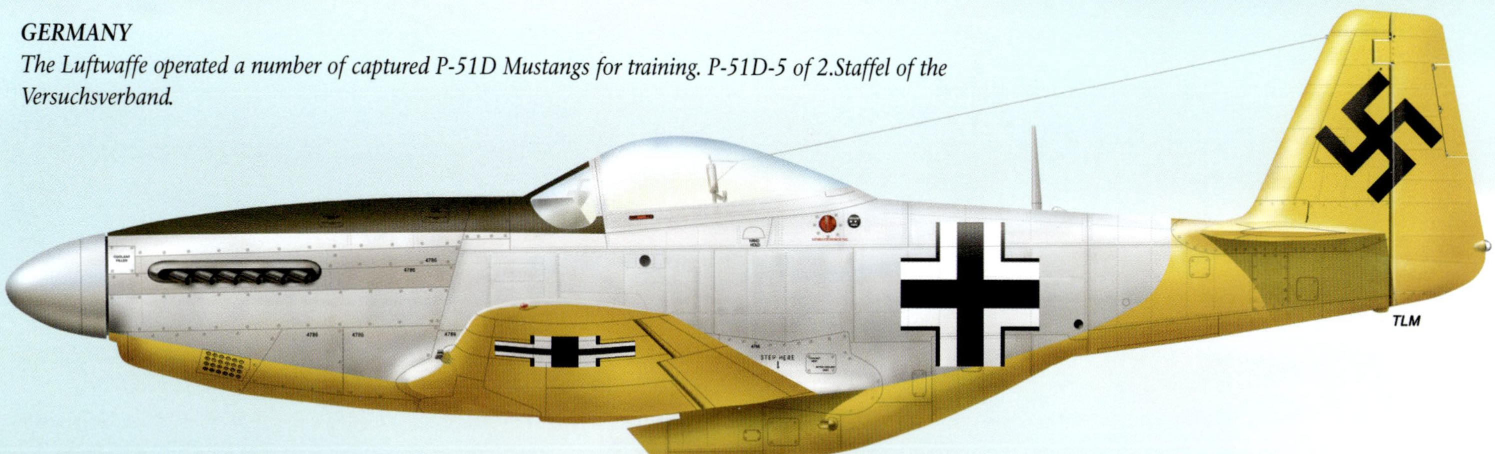

GUATEMALA

Fuerza Aerea Guatemalteca (FAG) acquired 20 F-51Ds starting from August 1954, and this number further increased later. The final count of Mustangs reaching Guatemala was officially 30, but additional F-51Ds may have been purchased from Israel. Mustangs were operated by the No.1 Fighter Squadron into the early 1970s, against guerrillas.

FAG P-51D of 1st FS, 1966.

HAITI

Haiti bought four or six P-51Ds just after WWII, and some of them remained in service into the 1960s.

Corps d'Aviation d'Haiti (Haitian Air Corps) P-51D with tactical no 916, circa 1963. Note F-86 drop tanks.

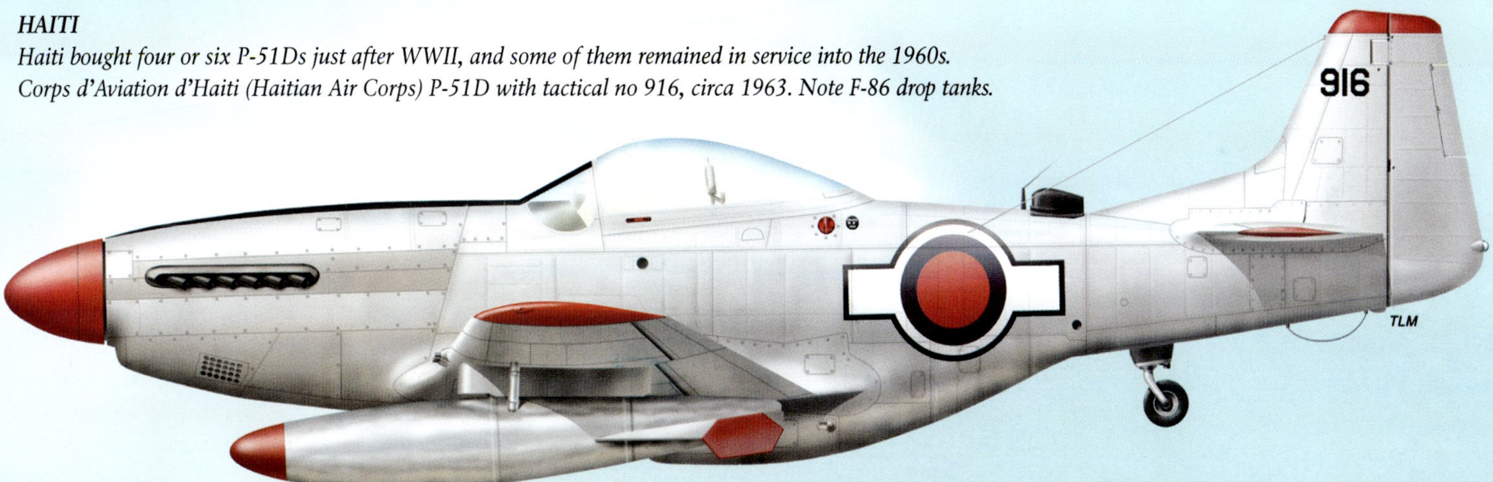

INDONESIA

Indonesia acquired some F-51s from the departing Netherlands East Indies Air Force in 1949/1950. The Mustangs were used against Commonwealth forces during the Indonesian confrontation in the early 1960s. P-51D, serial: F-324 (ex H-324) of 3 Skuadron, Angkatan Udara Republik Indonesia (AURI), in 1950-1962.

ISRAEL

Two P-51 Mustangs were illegally bought by Israel in 1948 for use in the War of Independence (1948). 25 additional aircraft were bought from Sweden in 1952 and Nicaragua but were replaced by jets at the end of the 1950s. P-51D, serial D-190 of 101 Tajeset (101st, Squadron), Israel Defense Force/Air Force (IDFAF), late 50s.

ITALY. *Aeronautica Militare Italiana (AMI), Italian Air Force was supplied with American equipment, including P-51Ds. An initial batch of 50 aircraft plus one two-seat conversion was issued in September 1947. The next batch to be allocated to the AMI in February 1949 contained 20 aircraft, again to be taken from storage in Germany. All aircraft of these deliveries were P-51D-20-NA – 32 aircraft and P-51D-25-NA – 38 aircraft. The next 100 aircraft were taken from storage in the U.S. and arrived by ship at Bridinsi harbor in 1950. These were: P-51D-25-NA – 56 aircraft, and P-51D-25-NT – 44 aircraft. 173 Mustangs were in total assigned to the AMI under MDAP.*
AMI P-51D, Serial: 4-12 (MM4300) of 4 Stormo, Circa 1952.

NETHERLANDS. *Before end of the war, the Netherlands received 40 P-51Ds for use by the Netherlands East Indies Air Force. They were operated by Nos 121 and 122 Squadrons. When the war against Japan ended, Dutch Mustangs were used in the Indonesian conflict. When Indonesia became independent on December 27, 1949, its air arm (the Angkatan Udara Republic Indonesia - AURI) was slated to receive two squadrons of F-51D Mustangs from the departing Dutch. In June of 1950, the Netherlands East Indies Air Force was officially disbanded and the surviving Mustangs were transferred to the AURI. P-51D-25-NT 'Evelyn' of 120 Squadron, ML-KNIL Serial: N3-630/H-330 (44-84793),1948. Formerly N3-622. Later reserialled as H-330 and finally transfered to AURI as F-330.*

NEW ZEALAND

In 1945, the Royal New Zealand Air Force decided to acquire 370 Mustangs, which were to be used in the final battle against Japan. The first batch was to consist of 30 P-51D-25-NT aircraft, with the remaining being P-51Ks.

The end of the war in the Pacific made the acquisition of 370 Mustangs by New Zealand unnecessary, and the order was cancelled. However, the 30 P-51D-25-NTs were already en-route. These aircraft were not placed in service, but were stored in the event of future need. In 1951, the New Zealand government decided to beef up the Territorial Air Force, a reserve component which had been revived after the war. The first four Mustangs entered service with No 4 Squadron of the TAF in late 1951.

NZ2413 at the end of its life with No.1 (Auckland) Squadron, after being struck off in October 1955. It had 36 inch roundels in six positions and seems to have been partially repainted silver at some stage with bare metal areas still showing around the Squadron badge and remaining stencils. Anti-glare panel is matt black.

(via Malcolm Laird)

NICARAGUA

Nicaragua took delivery of a few F-51Ds in 1947 and 26 Mustangs from Sweden in 1954. Some of them remained in service well into the 1960s. P-51D of Fuerza Aerea Nicaragua (FAN), serial unknown.

PHILIPPINES.

The Philippines received about 150 P-51 Mustangs after World War II. These became the backbone of the postwar Philippine Army Air Corps and Philippine Air Force and were used extensively during the Huk campaign, fighting against Communist insurgents. P-51D, code 001, circa 1947.

POLAND

In 1945, 303 (Polish) Squadron received 20 Mustang Mk IV/Mk IVA replacements. Postwar, between 6 December 1946 and 6 January 1947, all five Polish squadrons equipped with Mustangs were disbanded. Poland returned approximately 80 Mustang Mk IIIs and 20 Mustang Mk IV/IVAs to the RAF, which returned them to the U.S. government. Mustang IVA, KM112, PD•D, autumn 1945.

Right: *Mustang IVA, KM220 , RF•B just after delivery to 303 (Polish) Squadron, Andrews Field, 5 April 1945. Note that Polish national insignia and squadron badge has still not been painted on.*

(via ***Wojtek Matusiak****)*

SOMALIA.

From 1950 to 1960, Somalia was under Italian administration. Italy ran the "Corpo di Sicurezza della Somalia", which operated a few F-51D Mustangs. Eight of these aircraft were handed over to Somalia, when the the country was given independence. Mustangs remained in service until 1968.

SOUTH AFRICA

During Korean War, the South African Air Force committed its 2nd "Cheetah" Squadron to the United Nations effort. The "Cheetah" Squadron was equipped with loaned F-51Ds and was attached to the USAF's 18th Fighter Bomber Wing. 95 Mustangs were loaned to 2nd Squadron. F-51D, Serial: 335 of SAAF of 2 Sqn 'Flying Cheetahs', Pyongyang, Korea, 1952.

SOUTH KOREA

With the outbreak of the Korean War, 10 F-51D Mustangs were provided to the Republic of Korea Air Force (ROKAF) as a part of the "Bout One" Project. They were flown by both South Korean airmen as well as by U.S. advisers led by Major Dean Hess. Later, more Mustangs were provided both from USA and from South African stocks.

One of the most famous Korean Mustang, code number 18, flown by Col. Dean Hess. Formerly USAF serial 44-74692, it was assigned to the "Bout One" project on 8th October 1950. This F-51 D belonged to 1st Fighter Squadron, ROKAF.

(Stratus coll.)

SWEDEN

In February 1945, Sweden purchased 50 P-51Ds designated J 26, which were delivered by American pilots in April and assigned to the F 16 wing at Uppsala as interceptors. In early 1946, the F 4 wing at Östersund was equipped with a second batch of 90 P-51Ds. A final batch of 21 airplanes was purchased in 1948. In all, 161 J 26s served in the Swedish Air Force during the late 1940s. About a dozen were modified for photo reconnaissance and re-designated S 26.

(Photo ***Archive Svensk Flyghitorisk Förening****)*

SWITZERLAND

In December 1947, a contract was signed between the USA and Switzerland for the Swiss Air Force to receive 100 aircraft of the D-20 or D-25 version to be delivered as soon as possible, plus an additional 30 aircraft for use as spare parts. The first 26 aircraft were delivered in February 1948, and the last Mustangs arrived in August 1948. Mustangs were finally phased out of service in 1956.

Above: *P-51D-20-NA code J-2003 (USAAF s/n 44-72350) just after delivery to the Swiss Air Force.*
Below: *P-51D-20-NA code J-2063 (USAAF s/n44-64149) in Dark Green uppersurfaces. 9 Mustangs received camouflage in 1954.*

Mustang Mk IVA, KH653 of 19 Squadron, RAF in early 1945. KH655 was painted in ANA 613 Olive Drab, ANA 603 Sea Grey and ANA 602 Light Grey, with the forward part of the fuselage in yellow and the spinner in yellow with black bands.

UK

P-51D and K Mustangs were supplied to the RAF under Lend-Lease. An initial batch of 281 planes was delivered in 1944, and were designated Mustang IV by the RAF. They became standard equipment with Nos 19, 64, 65, 112, 118, 122, 154, 213, 149, 260, 303 (Polish), 306 (Polish), 442 and 611 Squadrons. 594 P-51Ks were also delivered to the RAF under the designation Mustang IVA. The serial numbers of the Mustang IVs supplied to the RAF were as follows: KH641/KH670 (P-51D), KH671/KH870 (P-51K), KM100/KM492 (P-51K), KM493/KM743 (P-51D), KM744/KM799 (not delivered), TK589 (P-51D 44-13332).

YUGOSLAVIA

P-51D-5-NA, serial: (44-13278), HL-L, "Weary Willie", ex 31st FG, USAAF. This aircraft was interned in 1945. Withdrawn from service in 1946.

URUGUAY

Uruguay received a few P-51Ds just after the war, and these remained in service until 1960, when they were replaced by F-80C Shooting Stars. 8 of the survivors were transferred to Bolivia. FAU, P-51D, code FAU-255 of Escuadrilla 1, Grupo 2 Blanco, Glendale, September 1950.